CAMBRIDGE TEXTS IN THE
HISTORY OF POLITICAL THOUGHT

———

SAMUEL PUFENDORF
*On the Duty of Man and Citizen According
to Natural Law*

CAMBRIDGE TEXTS IN THE
HISTORY OF POLITICAL THOUGHT

Series editors

RAYMOND GEUSS
Lecturer in Philosophy, University of Cambridge

QUENTIN SKINNER
Regius Professor of Modern History in the University of Cambridge

Cambridge Texts in the History of Political Thought is now firmly established as the major student textbook series in political theory. It aims to make available to students all the most important texts in the history of western political thought, from ancient Greece to the early twentieth century. All the familiar classic texts will be included, but the series seeks at the same time to enlarge the conventional canon by incorporating an extensive range of less well-known works, many of them never before available in a modern English edition. Wherever possible, texts are published in complete and unabridged form, and translations are specially commissioned for the series. Each volume contains a critical introduction together with chronologies, biographical sketches, a guide to further reading and any necessary glossaries and textual apparatus. When completed the series will aim to offer an outline of the entire evolution of western political thought.

For a list of titles published in the series, please see end of book

SAMUEL PUFENDORF

On the Duty of Man and Citizen According to Natural Law

EDITED BY

JAMES TULLY

Associate Professor of Political Science and Philosophy,
McGill University

TRANSLATED BY

MICHAEL SILVERTHORNE

Associate Professor of Classics, McGill University

CAMBRIDGE
UNIVERSITY PRESS

PUBLISHED BY THE PRESS SYNDICATE OF THE UNIVERSITY OF CAMBRIDGE
The Pitt Building, Trumpington Street, Cambridge, United Kingdom

CAMBRIDGE UNIVERSITY PRESS
The Edinburgh Building, Cambridge CB2 2RU, UK
40 West 20th Street, New York, NY 10011–4211, USA
10 Stamford Road, Oakleigh, VIC 3166, Australia
Ruiz de Alarcón 13, 28014 Madrid, Spain
Dock House, The Waterfront, Cape Town 8001, South Africa

http://www.cambridge.org

© Cambridge University Press 1991

First published 1991
Reprinted 1995, 1998, 2000

Printed in the United Kingdom at the University Press, Cambridge

British Library Cataloguing in Publication data

Pufendorf, Samuel, 1632–94
On the duty of man and citizen according to natural law. –
(Cambridge texts in the history of political thought)
I. Title II. Tully, James
171.2

Library of Congress cataloguing in publication data

Pufendorf, Samuel, Freiherr von, 1623–1694.
[De officio hominis et civis. English]
On the duty of man and citizen according to natural law /
Pufendorf: edited by James Tully: translated by Michael
Silverthorne.
p.   cm. – (Cambridge texts in the history of political
thought)
Translation of: De officio hominis et civis.
Includes bibliographical references (p.   ) and index.
ISBN 0 521 35195 2 (hardback). – ISBN 0 521 35980 5 (pbk.)
1. Natural law. 2. International law. 3. Political science.
I. Tully, James, 1946– . II. Silverthorne, Michael. III. Title.
IV. Series.

K457.P8D4313 1991
340´.1–dc20 90–20358 CIP

ISBN 35195 2 hardback
ISBN 35980 5 paperback

Contents

Main works by Pufendorf and abbreviations

EJU *Elementorum jurisprudentiae universalis libri duo.* Elements of universal jurisprudence in two books. 1660.

DRGP *De rebus gestis Philippi Amyntai filio.* On the history of Philip of Macedon. 1663. (In *DAS*.)

DSI *De statu imperii Germanici.* On the constitution of the German Empire by Severinus de Monzambano (Pufendorf). 1667.

DJN *De jure naturae et gentium libri octo.* On the law of nature and nations in eight books. 1672.

DOH *De officio hominis et civis juxta legem naturalem libri duo.* On the duty of man and citizen according to natural law in two books. 1673.

DAS *Dissertationes academicae selectiores.* Select scholarly essays. 1675.

SC *Specimen controversiarum.* A simple of controversies. 1677. Contains *De origine et progressu disciplinae juris naturalis.* On the origin and progress of the discipline of natural law. (In *ES*.)

HUP *Historische und politische Beschreibung der geistlichen Monarchie des Stuhls zu Rom.* A historical and political description of the spiritual monarchy of Rome. By Basilius Hyperta (Pufendorf). 1679. (In *EZDH*.)

EZDH *Einleitung zu der Historie der vornehmsten Reiche und Staaten so itziger Zeit in Europa sich befinden.* Introduction to the history of the principal realms and states as they currently exist in Europe. 1682–6.

ES *Eris Scandica, qua adversus libros de jure naturali et gentium objecta diluuntur.* Scandinavian polemics, in which the objections against the book *On the law of nature and nations are dissolved.* 1686. (Contains *SC.*)

CRS   *Commentariorum de rebus Suecicis libri XXVI ab expeditione Gustavi Adolphi in Germaniam ad abdicationem usque Christinae.* 1686. Tr. with DRC as *The compleat history of Sweden,* two volumes. 1702.

DHR   *De habitu religionis christianae ad vitam civilem. On the nature of religion in relation to civil life.* 1687.

DRF   *De rebus Friderici Wihelmi Magni Electoris Brandenburgici commentariorum libri XIX. On the history of the Great Elector, Frederick William of Brandenburg, in 19 books.* 1692.

JFD   *Jus feciale divinum sive de consensu et dissensu protestantium exercitatio posthuma. The law of covenants, or on the consensus and dissensus among Protestants.* 1695.

DRC   *De rebus a Carolo Gustavo Sueciae rege gestis commentariorum libri VII.* 1696. Tr. with CRS as *The compleat history of Sweden,* two volumes. 1702.

DRGF   *De rebus gestis Friderici III Electoris Brandenburgici. On the history of Frederick III, Elector of Brandenburg.* 1784.

Chronology of Pufendorf's life and publications

1632   8 January: born in the village of Dorchemnitz bei Thalheim, parish of Fiohe, Erzgebirge region of Saxony.

1650   Enters University of Leipzig to study Lutheran theology and develops interests in humanities, natural science and jurisprudence during six-year residence. Presents work on ancient constitutions and the origins of states (Döring 1988).

1656   Enters University of Jena and is granted a master's degree. In 1657 studies natural law and moral philosophy with Erhard Weigel (1625–99), whom he may have met earlier in Leipzig.

1658   Tutor to family of Peter Julius Coyet, Swedish minister in Copenhagen. Writes his first exposition of natural law, *Elements of universal jurisprudence*, while in prison as a result of war between Sweden and Denmark.

1659   Moves to Holland with Coyet family, recommended to Karl Ludwig, Elector Palatinate, by Peter de Groot, son of Hugo Grotius, and dedicates *EJU* to Karl Ludwig (pub. 1660).

1661   Accepts associate professorship of international law and philology, later renamed natural and international law, Faculty of Philosophy, University of Heidelberg, offered to him by Karl Ludwig, after the law faculty denies his request for a professorship in constitutional law.

1663   Writes study of Philip of Macedon, *On the history of Philip of Macedon* (pub. in *DAS*).

1664   Writes his controversial analysis of the Imperial constitution of Germany, *On the constitution of the German Empire*. Widely criticized, banned in German universities and condemned by the Pope.

1670   Takes up full professorship in natural and international law, Faculty of Law, University of Lund, offered to him by King Charles XI of Sweden (1660–97) in 1667.

1672   Publishes his major work of natural law philosophy, *On the law of nature and nations*, dedicated to Charles XI.

1673   Publishes abridgement of *DJN*, *On the duty of man and citizen according to natural law*, dedicated to the Chancellor of the University of Lund.

1675   Publishes *Select scholarly essays* in reply to his critics and in clarification of his theory.

1677   Publishes *A sample of controversies* and writes but does not publish until 1686 *Scandinavian polemics* in further clarification and reply to his critics.

1677   Moves to Stockholm after Danish army captures Lund (1676) and begins political career as privy councillor, secretary of state and royal historian to Charles XI.

1679   Publishes critical history of the Catholic Church and its claim to sovereignty, *A historical and political description of the spiritual monarchy of Rome*, under pseudonym Basilius Hyperta. (In *EZDH*.)

1682   Publishes (1682–6) his encyclopaedic work in comparative politics and international relations, a comparative analysis of the interests and powers of European states, *Introduction to the history of the principal realms and states as they currently exist in Europe*. Writes two works on contemporary Swedish history in this period in Stockholm.

1687   Publishes his theory of the relation of church to state in response to the revocation of the Edict of Nantes, 1685, *On the nature of religion in relation to civil life*, dedicated to the leader of Protestant Europe, Frederick William I, the Great Elector of Brandenburg – Prussia (1640–88).

1688 Moves to Berlin and begins career as court historian and privy and judicial councillor; first to Frederick William I and when he dies in 1688, to his son, Frederick III of Prussia (1688–1713).

1689 Begins histories of the reigns of his two new sovereigns, includes a commentary on the Glorious Revolution in England in his history of Frederick III, and states his views on Protestant Europe in *The law of covenants, or on the consensus and dissensus among Protestants* (pub. 1695).

1694 Travels to Sweden in the spring to publish his history of Charles X and to receive a barony from Charles XI. Dies on 26 October during return sea voyage to Germany.

Editor's introduction

Overview

As the preceding Chronology indicates, Pufendorf's writings fall into three groups.[1] The first is his attempt to construct a comprehensive political and moral philosophy appropriate to the conditions of modern Europe and based on a set of universal principles or natural laws. He began this project at the University of Jena and worked it out from 1658 to 1677 in the three texts on natural law (*EJU*, *DJN*, *DOH*), the analysis of the German imperial constitution (*DSI*), and the three collections of clarifications and replies to his critics (*DAS*, *SC*, ES). This enterprise is surveyed in the following four sections of the Introduction.

When Pufendorf moved from the University of Lund to Stockholm in 1677 as political adviser to the Swedish king Charles XI, he set aside the juristic analysis of politics in terms of universal law and obligation and turned to the major competing approach to the understanding of politics in the seventeenth century. This method consists in analysing the relations within and among contemporary European states by means of comparative and historical analyses of their interests and relative powers with a view to predictions and recommendations to state builders. From the *Reason of state* (1598) by Giovanni Botero (1540–1617) and the early Spanish and French *raison d'état*

---

[1] The use of non-sexist language to introduce Pufendorf's theory would cover over its gender bias, which needs rather to be exposed. Therefore, 'man' and male pronouns have been used to make explicit the exclusion of women from politics and their social subordination in the theory, and, in so doing, to facilitate criticism.

writers, this form of analysis was rapidly developed into pan-European sciences of comparative politics and international relations. The object domain of these sciences is the modern system of independent states locked into a military and commercial rivalry which emerged after the Thirty Years' War (1618–48) and the Peace of Westphalia (1648). Pufendorf's contributions include the earlier history of Philip of Macedon (*DRGP*), the political history of the Catholic Church (*HUP*), the contemporary political histories he wrote for Charles XI (*CRS, DRC*) and, after 1688, for Frederick William I and Frederick III of Prussia (*DRF, DRGF*), and especially his monumental introduction to the history of the principal states of Europe (*EZDH*). The *EZDH*, with its rigorous concepts of state interest and relative powers and its comprehensive design, was republished throughout the eighteenth century. The editors of the French editions added more chapters, making it a prototype of Enlightenment encyclopaedias of comparative politics.

The third group comprises Pufendorf's attempts to define the correct subordinate relation of religion to politics in Protestant states after the Peace of Augsburg (1555) recognized religious diversity within Christianity. These works were written in response to the revocation of the Edict of Nantes (1685) and the consequent division of Europe into two blocs: a Catholic bloc led by France and a Protestant alliance led by the rising Protestant hegemon, Frederick William of Prussia. They include *DHR, JFD* and his commentary on the Glorious Rebellion of 1688 in *DRGF*. The Protestant leaders perceived France to be aiming at – and succeeding in – the roll-back of the Protestant Reformation and the establishment of a European Imperial monarchy. William of Orange thus conquered England in 1688 in order to bring England into the Protestant balance, which was then mobilized in the Nine Years' War (1689–98), the first battle in a military and commercial contest that was to dominate European politics for 74 years. Consequently, Pufendorf's writings on the organization and defence of the Protestant religion were widely recognized as a leading presentation of the Protestant cause.

During the last eighteen years of his life, Pufendorf was adviser to three rulers who were seen as successful, modern, Protestant state-builders and exemplars of enlightened absolutism. His writings were thus taken to be philosophical presentations of modern, state-centred political practice. This association served to enhance the prestige his work rapidly acquired for its intellectual merit and to buttress its place at the centre of European political reflection for the next century.

The attention that Pufendorf's complex thought commanded in the European republic of letters in his lifetime and during the Enlightenment can be measured by the intellectual energy expended in responding to it by philosophers as diverse as John Locke (1632–1704), Gottfried Wilhelm Leibniz (1646–1716), Giambattista Vico (1668–1744), Gershom Carmichael (1672–1729), Christian Wolff (1679–1754), Francis Hutcheson (1694–1746), David Hume (1711–76), Jean-Jacques Rousseau (1712–78) and Adam Smith (1723–90). Moreover, even these now more familiar thinkers who challenged and repudiated certain lines of his thought came to accept other threads of it in the course of their criticisms and thereby wove these into the fabric of modern political thought.

Pufendorf's project

What is the collection of problems to which Pufendorf's natural law theory is a response? In his *On the origin and progress of the discipline of natural law* (in *SC* in *ES*) Pufendorf located his theory in the context of the writings of Hugo Grotius (1583–1645), John Selden (1585–1654), Thomas Hobbes (1588–1679) and Richard Cumberland (1631–1718). Jean Barbeyrac (1644–1720), who edited, annotated and translated into French *DJN* and *DOH*, prefaced his 1706 translation of *DJN* with an 'Historical and critical account of the science of morality' in which he added John Locke (1632–1704) to the list (Barbeyrac 1729). Recent scholars have called this 'the modern theory or school of natural law' and interpreted Pufendorf's theory in the light of its curriculum of shared problems. It has also been argued that the problems and solutions of this school continue to provide the stage setting for Rousseau, Hume, Smith, and German philosophers to Immanuel Kant (1724–1804). Others have suggested that the contractarian or juristic philosophy of John Rawls and Jurgen Habermas remains within the enduring conventions laid down by this modern school (see Bibliographical note).

Although the scholarship is too complex to summarize adequately here, it is possible to mention briefly three problems tackled by these authors and thus to facilitate understanding of Pufendorf's contribution. The first was to cleanse natural law of its grounding in the

Aristotelian and Thomistic concept of nature as a purposeful realm ordered by intrinsic teleological dispositions. This was believed to have been refuted by Galileo Galilei (1564–1642), Francis Bacon (1561–1626) and the circle of philosophers in correspondence with Merin Mersenne (1588–1648): Hobbes, Pierre Gassendi (1592–1655) and René Descartes (1596–1650). Therefore, the neo-Thomist natural law moral and political philosophy, shared by Dominican philosophers of the Catholic Reformation and Lutheran followers of Philipp Melanchthon (1496–1540) on the Protestant side, was claimed to be undermined as well. The philosophers of the new natural sciences advanced a concept of nature as a non-purposive realm of atoms on which God imposes, by an act of will, motion and an extrinsic order of efficient causes or regularities. The task of philosophers of natural law was henceforth to bring natural law into line with this scientific concept of nature and human nature (Tully 1988).

Pufendorf performs this task at the beginning of *DJN* and *DOH* 1.1–2 by setting forth morality and politics as the extrinsic imposition of moral concepts and laws by a superior on to an unordered realm of human movements that lack any intrinsic moral properties, and of human agents who lack any innate dispositions to moral and political life (Laurent 1982, Schneewind 1987). Hobbes and Locke share this imposition picture – or moral non-realism – to varying degrees. However, to take it as a defining feature of 'the modern school of natural law' is apt to be misleading since it is neither a sufficient nor a necessary condition of a modern natural law theory. The voluntarist tradition of natural law associated with William of Ockham shares this feature yet it predates this 'modern' school by 300 years. Conversely, one of the rival schools of natural law in the seventeenth century accepted the (limited) validity of the new form of explanation in the natural sciences yet went on to argue that this in no way undermines teleological explanation of human agency and the assumption that moral properties inhere in their objects (moral realism). Leibniz and the Cambridge Platonist Ralph Cudworth (1617–88) constructed modern neo-Aristotelian and neo-Platonic natural law philosophies in response to the revolution in the natural sciences. They argued that their reconstructions were invulnerable to criticisms launched by Mersenne's circle, criticized Hobbes and Pufendorf for reductively modelling moral and political philosophy on the new natural philosophy, and interpreted their theories as a continuation of the old voluntarism (Leibniz 1698, Lee 1702, Cudworth 1731). Barbeyrac in turn defended Pufendorf against Leibniz's criticism (Barbeyrac 1820).

Moreover, if the imposition premise is a defining feature of a school of natural law, then Grotius is not a member, yet Pufendorf, Barbeyrac and their modern commentators take him to. be the founder. Grotius wrote *On the laws of war and peace* (1625) prior to the publications of the Mersenne circle. In addition, he advances a dispositional account of human agency and a form of natural law realism.

The other two problems arose in connection with a decisive change in political practice. The practical situation Pufendorf faced was the unique political configuration that emerged in Europe as the outcome of the religious wars from the start of the Reformation to the end of the Thirty Years War. The Treaty of Westphalia became the authoritative initial interpretation of this configuration and thereby provided the framework for rival theories. The treaty recognized religious diversity (Catholic, Lutheran, Calvinist) within individual political units; granted supreme political power to territorial rulers within their domains and weakened the power of local estates; defined the German Empire as a kind of confederation of these independent principalities, each of which had the limited right to form alliances; and characterized Europe as a 'balance' of such independent political 'powers', kept in self-governing equilibrium by the alliance-building and occasional wars of the rulers, thus rendering superfluous the old pan-European authority of either papacy or empire. The problems of constructing a natural law theory of this complex configuration were religious and political.

Like Grotius and Hobbes, Pufendorf took the religious differences over which the wars had been fought to be irreconcilable. Hence, a new morality able to gain the consent of all Europeans to the new political order and bring peace would have to be independent of the confessional differences which divided them, yet also permit belief in and practice of these rival religions within the moral framework. The form of solution to this second problem was to derive a set of universal principles of right from two premises no person could reasonably doubt: a scientifically reconstructed condition common to all persons, the 'state of nature', and the empirically verifiable self-love or concern each person has with their own preservation (Seidler 1990). The first would free natural law from its dependency on the study of existing law codes and the Aristotelian starting point of commonly held opinions, and would thus emancipate it from the charge of relativism launched by Michel de Montaigne (1533–92) and Pierre Charron (1541–1603). The latter provided a good (preservation) which all could accept despite their disagreements over higher order goods, thus freeing the derivation of natural law from attachment to any particular religion (Zurbuchen 1986).

Pufendorf and Barbeyrac discerned these two premises in Grotius's theory and named him founder of the new school of natural law. Tuck and Seidler underscore these two similarities between Grotius and Pufendorf. Yet the dissimilarities are just as undeniable. Grotius builds his theory on the additional stoic premise of an innate disposition to love society for its own sake, whereas Hobbes opens *Of the citizen* with a refutation of this premise (translating it into oblique self-love) and takes this move to found a new science of politics. Pufendorf also denies the existence of such a teleological disposition to political society (but does not follow Hobbes's alternative). This feature of Pufendorf's philosophy – along with his imposition theory in contrast to Grotius's moral realism, his limitation of natural law to preservation, and his separation of natural law from religion – led his Aristotelian Lutheran critics to dispute his orthodoxy, deny his affiliation with Grotius, and to call him a follower of Hobbes and an atheist.

The third problem was political: to develop, within a framework of natural laws derived from these two premises, a theory of the consolidating independent political societies or states, the authority of rulers, and the duties and rights of subjects. Here again the solutions of the members of the school are diverse and contradictory because the circumstances in which they wrote were dissimilar in the following respect. Grotius and Hobbes wrote during the Thirty Years War. Grotius's objective was to regulate and limit by law the devastating warfare that then ruled Europe by force and rendered rule by law exceptional and epiphenomenal. Hobbes sought to construct and win allegiance to a strong unified state capable of putting an end to the rebellions that destroyed the weak, internally divided political agglomerations on which European civilization rested and put Europeans in a war of all against all.

Introduction

The political order established by the Peace of Westphalia subordinated war to politics and brought a general peace and stability that Grotius and Hobbes had only imagined. Pufendorf's generation was the first to experience and reflect on this modern political arrangement, the Westphalian system of sovereign states, that has literally constituted the enduring political foundation of the modern world through over 300 years of momentous economic, scientific and social change on the surface.

In the specific sense, therefore, of being the first to present a comprehensive theory of the existing European state system, Pufendorf is the first philosopher of modern politics. This reflective stance first appears in *DSI* (Denzer 1976). He categorically divides the Westphalian era from the world of war and devastation that preceded it, and he judges the extant organization of the German Empire and the Roman law terminology used to identify it to be monstrous and anachronistic relative to the standards and concepts appropriate to the new political order of independent states. His natural law theory, which imposes these standards and concepts on to the new order, throws a unique and fascinating light on the foundation of modern politics for two main reasons.

First, Pufendorf could view the modern political configuration from within its recently established boundaries *and* from the other world outside its boundaries – the preceding state of war and insecurity which he had experienced as a youth. He was able to draw on this dual experience to construct the two concepts which are used in a natural law philosophy to define each other by a series of contrasts: the state of nature as a world of war and insecurity and the state of political society as a world of general peace and security. The most compelling contrast is at *DOH*, II.1.9. For later theorists, on the other hand, the state of nature is the distant and imaginary horizon of their political thought and experience, available only through theoretical abstraction or conjectural history.

Second, the change in circumstances from the age of Grotius and Hobbes to the age of Pufendorf was accompanied by a change in theoretical perspective. The question underlying and orienting the thought of Grotius and Hobbes is how to establish political society and obedience to it out of the circumstances of devastating war and insecurity. The Westphalian settlement solved this problem in practice. Accordingly, the question which underlies and orients

Pufendorf's theory (and the theories which followed) is very different: how does one conduct oneself so as to become a useful member of such a society and polity (1.3.8 and 11.5.5). From this orientation, he could take what he wanted from Grotius and Hobbes and work these elements into a theoretical framework constructed to address the question at hand. As he makes clear in the Preface, his orientation and framework constitute a new *discipline* of natural law.

The demarcation argument

DOH is a compendium of Pufendorf's major work, *DJN*. In it he 'expound[s] to beginners the principal topics of natural law' (p. 6). It does not include his extensive arguments for each conclusion, nor his endlessly fascinating responses to rival views, nor his elaborate quotations from Classical, Christian, Roman law and contemporary sources. For this panorama one must turn to the larger work (*DJN*). Nonetheless, this shorter work is a genuine compendium: a short, complete summary of his whole political and moral philosophy. Furthermore, its clarity and succinctness render it both an independent statement of and a helpful guide to the unabridged version, where the density of elaboration occasionally obscures the central points. The philosophical precision of the text is attested to by the large number of philosophers who used it, rather than *DJN*, as the basis of their lectures, commentaries and polemics (Laurent 1982).

The book is dedicated to Count Gustav Otto Steenbock, Chancellor of the University of Lund, in return for the benefits he bestowed on Pufendorf in granting him tenurial protection from his critics (pp. 3–5). In all humility he cannot hope to match the benefits granted to him by his illustrious patron, but he can offer in reciprocal gratitude what such a noble person esteems – loyalty and devotion. The reciprocal performance of other-regarding social duties turns out on closer inspection to be advantageous to each party, thus illustrating for all to see the Senecan thesis of benevolence and gratitude on which his entire philosophy rests (1.3.7, *DJN*, 11.3.15).

Pufendorf states in the Preface that his aim is to expound the elements of natural law in a manner which is easy to learn and so 'to steep their [students'] minds in a moral doctrine whose usefulness in civil life is accepted as obvious' (p. 6). In publishing a practical, politico-moral manual Pufendorf is performing the civic duty he enjoins on all educators: to expound 'such doctrines as are consistent with the right purpose and usage of states, and [to ensure] that the citizens' minds be steeped in them from childhood' (II.7.8), and to 'avoid [teaching] all dogmas which tend to disturb civil society' (II.18.9).

Although the compendium was eventually adopted by the universities of Protestant Europe in the eighteenth century for this conservative purpose, the initial reception was hostile. The reason for the controversy can be seen in the razor-sharp demarcation of the discipline and practice of natural law which rounds off the Preface. It was presumably written in response to the first criticism of *DJN*: the *Index of certain novelties which Herr Samuel Pufendorf in his book on the law of nature and nations published at Lund against orthodox principles*, published in 1673 three months after *DJN*, by Nikolaus Beckmann, a professor of Roman law, and Josua Schwartz, a professor of theology (and Pufendorf's confessor), both at the University of Lund.

The demarcation argument circumscribes the field of natural law. Pufendorf demarcates the study and practice of natural law from civil jurisprudence and the institution of civil law on one side and from moral theology and divine law on the other. His practical point in doing this is to protect his theory from the criticisms of the lawyers and theologians by showing that their characteristic preoccupations are separate from the distinct realm of knowledge and of human action governed by natural law. The theoretical achievement this in turn brought about is to have constituted a distinctive juridical or law-centred discipline of moral and political philosophy. Unlike earlier and competing natural law theories, the field of study demarcated in the Preface is independent of the disciplines of legal studies and theology and possesses its own specific vocabulary, organized around Pufendorf's original concept of sociality (*socialitas*) and its cognates. This vocabulary brings to reflective awareness and partly constitutes a corresponding realm of human behaviour for study and governance – the social. Neither Grotius nor Hobbes, as Pufendorf, Barbeyrac, Tuck and Pufendorf's later critics all note, set out boundaries so clearly and drew contrasts so decisively.

Pufendorf demarcates the discipline of natural law by stating its six constitutive features and contrasting these with civil law and divine law (or moral theology). First, the subject matter of natural law is the set of universal social duties common to all mankind, 'those which render him capable of society [*sociabilis*] with other men', whereas civil law treats the legal duties of particular states and moral theology, the duties of particular religions such as Christianity (p. 7). Second, the ground of justification of natural laws is that they are demonstrated by reason 'to be essential to sociality [*socialitas*] among men', whereas civil laws are derived from the will of the sovereign and divine laws from the will of God (p. 7). Here he repeats his novel view: it is 'sociality . . . which we have laid out as the foundation of natural law' (p. 12). Third, the method of discovery of natural law is unaided reason; that of divine law is revelation (p. 7). Fourth, the scope or aim of natural law is to conduct man in the human court 'to become a useful [*commodum*] member of human society' (1.3.8) – natural law 'forms man on the assumption that he is to lead this life in society with others' – whereas divine law in the divine court aims to form man for salvation in the next world (p. 8). Fifth, the ethical material over which natural law has jurisdiction is for the most part 'men's external action' only; divine law governs inner thoughts, intentions and desires as well (p. 9). Sixth, the condition of human nature which natural law takes as given is man as he is after the Fall: corrupt, inclined to self-love and 'seething with evil desires' (p. 10). Moral theology must treat man in both a corrupt and an uncorrupted condition.

It is not difficult to understand why this orientation and framework struck the immediate audience as a prescription for anarchy and impiety (as Beckmann and Schwartz put it) and why it took some time for Europeans to adjust to it as the ground plan for civil peace in modern Europe. Yet it is equally obvious how it aims to solve the problem of finding a morality (or, better, a sociality) capable of uniting a confessionally divided Europe by freeing natural law morality from any attachment to confessional differences. Its failure in Catholic Europe, let alone in non-Christian societies, belies its university.

In sum, the six steps in the demarcation argument transform natural law morality into a *social* theory, concerned exclusively with ordering the external actions of self-loving men by social duties which render them useful members of society. As Leibniz typically commented, this eliminates, and cuts natural law philosophy off from, the essential concerns of any known or practicable moral system, either Classical or Christian: namely, other types of duty, cultivation of character and virtues, governance of the inner life of intentions, desires and motives, and the development of moral and religious aspirations which transcend sociality (Leibniz 1706). Pufendorf's point is that only if these traditional concerns are eliminated from the publicly enforced morality, left to various church and moral authorities, and natural law reoriented to the realm of sociality, will civil peace and social life be secure.

Theorists from Locke to Kant came to accept and to conventionalize Pufendorf's initially heterodox discipline and to build on it social theories of toleration, pluralism, commercial progress and freedom, far removed from Pufendorf's basic concern with peace and order. As a result, later generations have tended to take it for granted and so overlook the decisive role Pufendorf played in establishing the juridical form of modern thought that a contemporary philosopher has called 'morality – the peculiar institution' (Williams 1985).

Sociality and utility

The aim of the compendium is to show how corrupt men can conduct themselves as social beings in their outward actions, and thus be able to live in society with others. The way Pufendorf does this is to expound, in the terms of the six demarcative features of natural law theory and practice, the duties the performance of which constitutes being a good member of human society. In Book I he sets out the duties that apply to all men and, in Book II, those that apply to men as members of basic and universal forms of human societies: the state of nature, the family, the economic unit of masters and slaves, and the state. Two chapters are fundamental. In I.3 the basis of all social duties is explained and in II.5 the formation of states, rulers and citizens is set forth and the point of his theory stated: the performance of the duties which sustain this political ensemble is the necessary condition for any but the most rudimentary form of social existence.

In I.1.1 duty (*officium*) is defined as 'human action in conformity with the commands of law on the ground of obligation'. Pufendorf maps out the conditions of voluntary human action, since all duties are voluntary (I.2.4), and shows that (contrary to the moral realists) the understanding, the passions, and the free will possess no sources of orderliness and give rise to a chaos of amoral action. To avoid the confusion and disorder that would have followed, he continues in I.2, it was necessary that some moral rule should be imposed from the outset to which the will could be made to conform (1.2.1) and with reference to which otherwise amoral actions could be evaluated and named (1.2.11). 'Rule' is then identified with 'law', and 'law' with a 'decree by which a superior obliges one who is subject to him to conform to the superior's prescript' (1.2.2). Even one's basic sense of right and wrong is said to be acquired by being under the obligation of a law (1.2.4). This neatly encapsulates the imposition theory of *DJN* that proved to be both so controversial and so influential.

The third and final term in the definition of duty, obligation, is then explained as based on two conditions: a superior with the power to enforce his decree and a subject with good reasons to obey. The reasons are that obedience is beneficial, that the superior means well and is able to care for the subject better than himself, and that obedience is voluntary (1.2.4–5). Obligation turns on fear of punishment, as with Hobbes, and on respect for the benevolence of the superior, as with the stoics, thereby making benevolence–gratitude constitutive of every social duty. Pufendorf immediately shows that the natural law duties meet all these conditions: they are voluntary, discovered by reason, the decrees of a superior, God, who enforces them with the rewards and punishments of heaven and hell, and whose benevolence and care constitute good reasons for obedience (1.2.6, 1.2.16, 1.3.10). (For objections and replies see Leibniz 1706, Barbeyrac 1820, Palladini 1978, Schneewind 1987, Moore and Silverthorne 1989).

In 1.3.1–7 the ground of justification of natural law – sociality – is derived from 'the common character and condition of mankind' (1.3.1). In particular, the conclusion that 'in order to be safe, it is necessary for him to be sociable [*sociabilis*]' (1.3.7; *cf.* 1.2.16, 1.3.10), is derived from six irreducible features of the human condition. Man's first concern is, as the stoics taught, his own conservation and well-being; yet his weakness (*imbecillitas*) and wretchedness render him incapable of securing either by his own efforts. Consequently, he needs to join with others in a social life of mutual assistance to gain what he wants. Although he is capable of engaging in social life, when he tries to associate out of self-regard an unlimited number of passions flare up and drive him to distrust, insolence, enmity, the infliction of harm and injury, and so to war. As a result, it is necessary not only to join together in order to meet the first three features, as Grotius and Hobbes taught, but also to do so in a form of life that prevents the anti-social friction of association (which Grotius and Hobbes overlooked). The only form of association which takes into account these six features and solves the social problem is for a man to be sociable with others in precisely the strategically other-regarding manner defined in 1.3.7 and laid down as the basis of natural law at 1.3.8: to 'join forces' and 'so conduct himself towards them that they are not given even a plausible excuse for harming him, but rather become willing to preserve and promote his advantages [or 'benefits': *commoda*]' (*cf. DJN* II.3.15).

Accordingly, the fundamental law of nature under which all others are subsumed is that every man ought to 'cultivate and preserve sociality' (*colendam et servandam esse socialitatem*) (1.3.9). This involves duties to God (1.4), to oneself (1.5) and to others (1.6ff.). Further, the subsumptive laws of nature that teach a man how to conduct himself in a manner which takes into account the effect of his actions on the actions of others in order 'to become a useful member of human society' (1.3.8) comprise three types of duty. First are the negative service duties of not injuring others, as Grotius and Hobbes had correctly discerned (1.6). However, these are insufficient. To eliminate the occasion of anti-social reaction it is also necessary to act towards others in a manner which evinces recognition of and displays respect for their equality of dignity as men, so that their highly sensitive and easily provoked self-esteem is not injured (1.7). This thesis that modern society also needs to rest on the mutual recognition of the equal dignity of all men, as opposed to the feudal and Renaissance honour ethic based on inequality (1.7.3), is one of Pufendorf's most profound and consequential insights (*DJN*, III.2). Third, to prevent ingratitude and the socially destructive spiral of behaviour it triggers, and to promote in others the countervailing dispositions of trust, gratitude and a willingness to reciprocate, it is necessary to perform duties of benevolence (1.8). The three types of duty provide the framework for the analysis of duties involved in contracts, agreements, oaths, property relations and language use (1.9–17), as well as of duties in families and states (Book II); and many of these are drawn from Roman law.

Although all three types of duty are necessary to preserve and cultivate the form of society in which a man can secure the conservation and well-being he cherishes, Pufendorf lays emphasis on the second and third. He does so partly because his predecessors failed to take them into account in their minimalist theories of natural negative service duties and natural rights of self-preservation. The deeper explanation is that they are designed to eliminate what for Pufendorf (following Seneca *On benefits*, IV.18), as for Shakespeare in *King Lear* (1608), is the primary cause of the dissolution of society and the descent into madness and war: the passion 'more odious and more detestable' than 'injustice' (I.8.8) – the 'monster ingratitude' (*King Lear*, I.5.37).

A number of critics charge that Pufendorf bases natural law on utility or interest (*utilitas*), not sociality (Palladini 1978, Barbeyrac 1729, *DJN*, II.3.15n). This is a misunderstanding. The performance of social duties has 'clear utility' (I.3.10) since the sociality this cultivates and preserves is the enabling condition of individual security and well-being (*cf. DJN*, II.3.16). However, the duties demanded by sociality frequently over-ride actions dictated by considerations of one's own immediate utility or expediency, and even involve a readiness to risk one's life for the sake of sociality (I.5, II.5.4, II.13.2, II.18.4). (Consequently, the first duty to oneself is to make oneself a useful member of society, I.5.1). Hence Pufendorf, following Cicero, carefully distinguishes between rational or long-term utility and depraved or short-term utility and argues that social duties are consistent with, but not based upon, the former (*DJN*, II.3.10). Actions based on the latter are inconsistent with sociality and, for this reason, self-defeating. If it is made the measure of right, as with Hobbes's subjective right of self-preservation, the society in which man would be able to achieve even his basic security would never evolve (*DJN*, II.3.11, II.3.16).

In *On the natural state of men*, written in 1675, Pufendorf again contrasts his theory with Hobbes's and finally abandons his attempts to distinguish two senses of utility, thus freeing his theory from any necessary connection to utility. He says the rational sense of utility has passed from common usage and the spurious sense, in which utility is defined in contrast to both socially fitting and regard for others, has gained exclusive sway (thereby explaining his critics' misunderstanding) (Seidler 1990: no. 10, p. 95L, p. 122E).

Henceforth, as he replies to Beckmann, 'the basic premise from which I draw the principles of natural law [sociality] stands in direct opposition to the theory of Hobbes [based on a right of self-preservation]. For I come very close to the reasonable system of the stoics, whereas Hobbes serves up a rechauffé of Epicurean theories' (*ES*). Finally, the theory of sociality is clearly constructed with reference to the passage on society and gratitude in Seneca's *On benefits*, iv.18, quoted in *DJN*, ii.3.15:

> By what other means are we preserved but by the mutual assistance of good turns? This commerce and intercourse of kindness adds strength and power to life; and, in case of sudden assaults, puts it into a better condition of defence. Take us all asunder and what are we but an easy and unequal prey to wild beasts? Man by nature is weak on every side: society fortifies his infirmity and arms his nakedness. Those two excellences, of reason and of society, render him the most potent of all creatures, who would otherwise be obnoxious to injuries from everything about him. Thus, by the help of union, he commands the world, who, if divided, would scarce be a match for any living rival. And it is society alone which gives him his sovereign sway over inferior creation. This was the thing which first restrained the violence of diseases, which lent crutches and support to old age, and administered consolation to grief. Take away this, and you cut asunder the bond of union, the vital string of mankind.

Grotius cites the same passage, but he interprets it to involve a natural disposition to love society for its own sake (*appetitus societatis*), in addition to self-love (*DJB*, Prel. dis. 8 n.2). Hobbes denies this: 'we do not . . . by nature seek society for its own sake, but that we may receive some honour or profit from it' (*Of the citizen*, p. 42). Pufendorf accepts Hobbes's argument while rejecting what Hobbes does with it. As a result, for Pufendorf, the passage from Seneca does not make reference to a social disposition, but rather it encapsulates the six features of the human condition that conjointly render society necessary. Although this conjunction furnishes man with good reasons to be social, the narrow motive of self-love leads him to enmity instead, as Pufendorf is the first to point out (I.3.5–6). Even the love of humanity that he claims is a natural sympathy for others, while important, is too weak to temper this bleak picture (I.8.1, II.1.11). To bring man's selfish motivation in line with his strategically other-regarding social duties, and so his rational utility, the benevolent Christian God enforces duties through fear of his punishments (I.3.10–13). Since belief in a benevolent and punishing God is thereby a necessary condition of social life (1.3.13), duties to God are the first of the social duties (1.4).

Nonetheless, Pufendorf is astute enough to observe that if men are unable to move themselves to perform the three types of duty by considering the earthly benefits that would thereby accrue to them, they are evidently not going to do much better by considering longer-term heavenly punishments or mild stings of conscience (II.5.9). So the system of sociality is incomplete because it lacks an effective means of enforcement. The missing remedy is found in Book II, where he explains that 'the effective remedy for suppressing evil desires, the remedy perfectly fitted to the nature of man, is found in states [*civitates*]' (II.5.9).

States and citizens

Book II opens with a distillation of Pufendorf's rich and unsurpassed analysis of the state of nature: the natural condition of mankind outside or prior to the establishment of states (see Denzer 1972, Seidler 1990). He defines it by three contrasts: in a condition of obedience to God versus the life of other animals; alone and weak versus the life of co-operation in states; and without political subjection versus subjection in states. In these conditions men are able to form into small associations of patriarchal families, in which women are naturally subject to men, and thus arise the duties of husbands and wives (II.2), parents and children (II.3), and masters and servants (II.4).

The primary reason why these associations are able to support only a rudimentary level of sociality is the absence of security (II.1.9). Without a common political authority the male heads of families are in a state of 'self-government'. They must attempt to enforce duties and settle disputes on an ad hoc and voluntary basis (II.1.8–10). Given the nature of man (here drawing on 1.3.1–7 and adding an antipathy to subjection at II.5.4) and the ineffectiveness of the threat of divine punishment (II.5.9), self-government fails and all are exposed to the threat of attack. The ensuing and engulfing conditions of suspicion and distrust outside households prevent the mutual trust necessary for the strategically rational actor to be willing to perform and promote other-regarding social duties. '[W]ar, fear, poverty, nastiness, solitude, barbarity, ignorance, [and] savagery' follow (II.1.9; *cf.* II.5.6), and the rational are forced to prepare for war (II.1.11).

It follows neatly from this scenario that states are established to provide security out of conditions of battle. The motivating reason which actually causes men to set up states is 'to build protection around themselves against the evils that threaten man from man' (II.5.7). Presumably drawing on his experience of the Thirty Years War, he states that it is not any Aristotelian love of society that moves men to form states (II.5.2); the savage conditions of war provide the impelling cause (*causa impulsiva*) that propels these self-loving animals into setting up states (II.5.6–7). States remove the cause of insecurity, and so lay the foundation for sociality among family heads, by uniting conflicting wills into one will and the powers of men into a power capable of effectively inflicting punishment on those who resist the common interest in security (II.5.9, II.6.4–6).

Although men set up states to serve their interest in security, as in Hobbes's theory, once they become members of states, men are bound to serve the state and to subordinate their good (life, wealth, fortune) to the good of the state, and even to identify their good with the state's, as in Cicero's theory. This is what it means to be a political animal: a good citizen or ruler (II.5.4–5, II.6.9, II.7.3, II.11.3, II.17.11, II.18.4). Pufendorf does not mean that the citizens' motivation is changed. This would contradict stipulation six of the demarcation argument. Rather, the system of laws legislated and enforced in a political community governs the citizens' conduct so that it serves to preserve and promote the public good (II.11.4). Since the preservation of this political order is the indispensable means to sociality, and since the obligation to promote sociality entails the obligation to promote the means to it (I.3.9), it follows that men are obliged by God and natural law to perform their political duties (II.6.14). Furthermore, since the performance of political and social duties sustains the order in which individual security and the benefits of society can be attained (II.5.7), it is a matter of one's rational utility to obey (II.5.8–9).

There are three ways in which men become useful members of states. First, they are constrained to obey civil laws by the 'fear of punishment' from civil authority (II.5.5, II.12, II.13). The legal system enforces the social duties of Book I (II.12.3–7), including the core duties to God (II.11.4). Second, citizens' minds and opinions are moulded by the family and public authorities in doctrines conformable with the ends of the state and by censorship of contrary doctrines (II.7.8, II.18.9). The third and most effective way is Pufendorf's original and often-copied modernization or socialization thesis summarized in the two parts of II.5.7 (which correspond to the two parts of the definition of sociality at 1.3.7). By establishing states initially for security, men provide the political base for and set in motion a self-developing social system of mutually beneficial duties in which the participants are, willy-nilly, progressively civilized and socialized (see Hont 1987).

In Book II, chapter 6 Pufendorf explains how a multitude (*multitudo*) of men are able to constitute an association or union (*coetus, populus*), a form of government (*regimen, respublica*), supreme authority or sovereignty (*summum imperium*), a ruler (*imperans*) or sovereign (*summum imperans*), subjects or citizens (*subditi, cives*), and a state (*civitas*). This chapter and the corresponding *DJN*, VII.2 comprise the most discriminating analysis of these seven concepts in early modern Europe and set forth the basic vocabulary for almost all later contract theories.

The activity of constituting a state consists in two agreements and one decree (II.6.1–9). First, a multitude of male heads of family, each with his independent will and judgement in the insecure state of nature, unanimously agree with each other to form a single and perpetual association and to administer their safety by common counsel and leadership. This first agreement constitutes an association or union (*coetus*) (II.6.7). Unlike the aggregate multitude of males who form it, the members of the association are bound together by the majority principle and the institutions necessary for their security. It also must be large enough to defend its members against existing states and empires (*DJN*, VII.2.7). The majority then decrees which form of government is appropriate to the task (II.6.8; discussed in II.7). Finally, a reciprocal agreement of sovereignty and subjection is required to constitute the single man or assembly on whom the government of the 'infant state' is conferred, and under what conditions (II.6.9; discussed in II.9.5–7), and all the others become subjects or 'citizens'. The agreement involves a reciprocal obligation: the citizens individually agree with the ruler to obey him, thereby taking on a range of civic duties (II.18.2–5), and the ruler agrees 'to care for the state' and to exercise supreme authority in accordance with the decree and only for the sake of common security and safety (II.6.9, II.11.3; *DJN*, VII.2.8).

Only when the second agreement is put into effect 'does a complete and regular state come into being' (II.6.9). The state, which men have created out of the union of their wills and powers, is a single living man with its own name, rights and possessions (II.6.10). After Hobbes, this is one of the first and clearest formulations of a specifically modern concept of the state: that is, a unified structure of will and power that incorporates and is independent of both the rulers and the subjects who bring it into being and become its constituents (for this concept see Skinner 1989). In *DJN* Pufendorf underscores the uniqueness and significance of this male creation of the masculine world of politics by quoting with approval Hobbes's depiction of it in the Introduction to *Leviathan*. By their agreements men create a state (*civitas*), an 'artificial man' with the virile attributes of strength, unity and unaccountability, of which they become the living members; just as God, by 'that divine command, "Let there be" or "Let us make men" . . . created the world' (VII.2.13). (For a feminist refutation, see Shelley 1818 and Mellor 1989.)

Although Pufendorf endorses Hobbes's concept of the state, in *DJN*, VII.2.9–12 he immediately explains that his account of the two agreements and one decree is a direct refutation of Hobbes's erroneous theory of state formation and a presentation of the correct theory. These arguments remain the best criticisms of Hobbes's theory.

According to Pufendorf, Hobbes eliminated both the traditional agreement to form an association and the reciprocal agreement of sovereignty and subjection because he saw that they were easily used to derive an 'excuse for rebellion' by 'those seditious men who in former years endeavoured to circumscribe royal power, and to place it under the control of subjects, or even to do away with it altogether' (*DJN*, VII.2.9). However, since these two agreements were the shared premises of both proponents of royal sovereignty and proponents of mixed or popular sovereignty, Hobbes's attack on them (on the correct observation that they were more favourable to the latter than the former) constituted a repudiation of the common ground on which the whole early modern contractarian controversy over sovereignty rested.

Hobbes then replaced both agreements with a single agreement of a multitude of men among themselves to submit to a ruler who is not part of nor subject to the agreement. He believed that this premise would place the sovereignty of the ruler on an incorrigible foundation and eliminate the possibility of justifying rebellion. The people as a corporate body cannot advance any kind of claim to limit the sovereign ruler because the single agreement avoids the formation of such a union or association. Second, the subjects cannot claim that the 'agreement between king and citizen is reciprocal, and that when the former does not keep the promises he made by an agreement, the latter are freed from obedience' (*DJN*, VII.2.9) because Hobbes's single agreement avoids a reciprocal agreement altogether.

Against Hobbes, Pufendorf reasserts the necessity of an agreement to form an initial association of the people and shows that Hobbes's rather contrived attacks on it are unsuccessful (*DJN*, VII.2.12). Then he points out that Hobbes's single agreement is fatally flawed. Since the subjects agree with each other to obey, rather than with the sovereign, if one man 'does not render obedience, all the rest would be free of' their obligation (*DJN*, VII.2.11).

Pufendorf's next line of argument is that a properly formulated reciprocal agreement does not provide an excuse for rebellion. 'Nor indeed, when we admit the existence of an agreement between ruler and citizens, do these inconveniences necessarily follow, which Hobbes seemed to have had before his eyes' (*DJN*, VII.2.10). First, he construes the two agreements and one decree as 'creating' supreme authority (*DJN*, VII.3.1) and the agreement of subjection as simply conveying its exercise – 'the government of the state' – to the ruler (II.6.10). Therefore, unlike doctrines of corporate popular sovereignty, the people, although it possesses unity, never possesses supreme authority and so cannot be said to 'delegate' it to a ruler and repossess it if the ruler breaks the agreement. Further, unlike doctrines of individual popular sovereignty, he stipulates that men do not possess the powers to punish and to legislate (the two attributes of supreme authority) in the state of nature and so they cannot repossess them if the agreement is violated (as in Locke's theory). Nor is supreme authority derived in any manner from their natural right of self-defence (as in Hobbes's theory; *DJN*, VIII.3.1–2). The thesis that supreme authority is created – simply by the subordination of one's will and the application of one's power to what the ruler decrees for common security (*DJN*, VII.2.5) – removes the shared convention that was so favourable to populist conclusions: that supreme authority must be transferred in some way by the reciprocal agreement.

Second, given that the ruler and subject are under a reciprocal obligation, how is the constitutive relation of governance between them defined so it does not provide a legitimate 'excuse for rebellion'? Following Grotius very closely, Pufendorf argues that the relation of sovereign and subject is like the relation of master and servant, or father and voluntarily adopted child, in the sense that the ruler has the authority to define what the subject is to do and to compel him to do it in matters of common security, whereas the subject possesses no such authority (*DJN*, VII.2.10; *DOH*, II.9.4; Grotius, *DJB*, 1.3.6–10). Although obligation is reciprocal, subjection is one-sided: the civil authority is unaccountable (II.9.2). This master and servant relation is meant to displace popular sovereignty and the other theory that Grotius had subjected to a relentless attack: that neither the ruler nor the ruled is sovereign, but rather they stand in a relation of 'mutual subjection' (in federal, mixed or balanced government; Grotius, *DJB*, 1.3.9). Indeed, in using 'subject' and 'citizen' interchangeably, and equating citizenship with servitude, Pufendorf's aim is to efface this whole early modern tradition in which citizens by definition share in political authority in some way or another, or possess political liberty (II.6.13; *DJN*, VII.2.20; Skinner 1989).

Pufendorf then asks if there are any circumstances in which citizens may resist a ruler who violates his obligation to defend his subjects, administer justice and preserve the state (*DJN*, VII.8.4). Citizens must either flee from the injuries committed by their ruler or passively bear them, including being killed, and they cannot assist innocent people who are pillaged, raped or murdered by their ruler (*DJN*, VII.8.5; *DOH*, II.9.4). Further, they cannot resist a ruler who over-rides justice in the interests or necessities of state (*DJN*, VII.8.6).

However, following Grotius again, he allows one exception in the case of tyranny: 'a people, can defend itself against the extreme and unjust violence of its prince' and, if successful, may set up a new ruler, just as a servant can resist such a master (*DJN*, VII.8.7; Grotius, *DJB*, 1.4.7). This act of 'a people or individuals' is not to be confused with the exercise of political authority, as it is by theorists of popular sovereignty and mutual subjection, but solely as the duty of self-defence (derived from 1.5). On the other hand, theorists of royal sovereignty are equally wrong to conclude that the lack of any political authority in the people leaves them defenceless, for one cannot assume that the original contractors 'wished to lay upon all the burden that they shall choose to die, rather than under any circumstances to repel with arms the unjust violence of superiors' (*DJN*, VII.8.7). This is a clever solution but, just as English radicals were able to exploit Grotius's similar argument, it seems to provide an open-ended 'excuse for rebellion' on the grounds of self-defence (Barbeyrac, for example, links Pufendorf to Sidney and Locke in his note to VII.8.7). Perhaps this is why it does not appear anywhere in *DOH*.

A strong and coherent state, Pufendorf argues, must have a unified and centralized arrangement of power and authority. This is a 'regular' state (II.8.2; *DJN*, VII.5.13). States which lack this are 'irregular' and, consequently, weak, incoherent and prone to disorder (II.7.9, II.8.12; Denzer 1976). This normative contrast serves, respectively, to legitimate the centralizing policies of the builders of absolutist, unified and modern states for whom he worked and wrote, and to stigmatize as 'irregular' the policies of his major opponents – the defenders of mixed, balanced or federal arrangements of political authority. Since these theorists of mutual subjection distribute political authority among the monarchy and various representative bodies, each of which is mutually subject in a variety of overlapping ways, they reject Grotius's and Pufendorf's principle of sovereignty, that political power is located in one place and is unaccountable (II.9.1–3), and they do not recognize the concept of the state as an entity independent of government. Thus, the only place their theories can be expressed in Pufendorf's political vocabulary is in the residual, pejorative and distorting category of irregular states.

The section on irregular states (II.8.12) is the distillation of a long argument against mixed and balanced government in *DJN*, VII.5.12–15. Recognizing that Aristotle is taken to be the founder of this tradition, he argues that Aristotle is not a theorist of mixed political authority, but rather of healthy and unhealthy variations of forms of government and types of administration within the background framework of unified sovereignty, much as Pufendorf himself proceeds (II.8.3–11). By locating his highly contested concept of supreme authority behind the debate, as part of the stage-setting since the time of Aristotle, he makes it appear that his opponents accept it too; just as placing the same concept as the backdrop to the debate over absolute and limited government makes it seem that everyone accepts it (II.9.5–6). But, in fact, it is precisely this concept of supreme authority that his opponents were contesting and seeking to limit and balance by overlapping mutual subjection (criticized in *DJN*, VII.5.13). For Pufendorf, this is a recipe for disorder, the prime example of which is the antiquated German Empire, and the scheme of the old warrior nobility, whose independence must be broken by the monarch (*DJN*, VII.5.15, referring to *DSI*, and VIII.4.15–30). Nonetheless, the prudent and benevolent sovereign respects the limits placed upon him by the original contractors and rules in accordance with the advice and counsel of wise and judicious citizens.

As Leibniz commented on Hobbes's theory, the effect of Pufendorf's theory of state formation is almost to efface his opponents' views and the political formations they defended. He presents a captivating picture of 'regular' states established by patriarchs in some distant state of nature, thereby hiding from view the actual struggle to consolidate such centralized and abnormal states during the seventeenth century in military opposition to the 'irregular' motley of criss-crossing and overlapping political authorities. These irregular political arrangements had governed Europeans for centuries and they were not completely swept away by the process of regularization. Not even France, the most unified state in Europe, approximated to the unrealistic representation of the state advanced by Hobbes and Pufendorf (Leibniz 1677).

Finally, the duty of the ruler is to bring about 'the safety of the people' and to achieve this he must place the good of the state above his own good (II.11.3). Pufendorf redescribes the duty of the ruler in the neostoic terms of 'dignity and tranquillity (or peace)' (II.7.2). Tranquillity internal to a state comprises four dimensions of security that were absent in the state of nature: security of life, limb and property by the administration of justice (II.7, II.11); security of souls by the protection and promotion of 'the pure and sincere Christian doctrine' (II.11.4); security of material well-being by mercantile policies and welfare for the disabled (II.11.11); and security of self-esteem and reputation by the ruler's distribution of honours (II.14). The last is important because the ruler must always treat citizens with respect for their dignity and distribute honours appropriately if he is to avoid the ingratitude and enmity analysed in 1.3 and 1.7 (II.14.15–16; *DJN*, VIII.4).

The ruler is also obligated to protect the people from external attack by means of diplomacy, alliance building, war-preparation and war-fighting (II.16, II.17). States are in the state of nature with each other, thereby constrained to act defensively, not benevolently, on the expectation that friendly states may become enemies, that peace may become war, and hence even in peace one must prepare for war (II.1.11). Hence, in addition to promoting the 'virtues of peace' the sovereign must also cultivate the 'virtues of war' (*DJN*, VIII.4; *DOH*, II.11.13): foster courage through compulsory military training, set up a permanent military establishment with sufficient revenue, and organize economic and welfare policies so they increase the overall strength of the state relative to its neighbours (II.11.3, II.11.11, II.18.4; see McNeill 1982 for these aspects of early modern state building). Consequently, rulers of states are compelled by the causal constraints of the interstate system to order the external actions of citizens in accordance with the logistical demands of anticipated battle without, at the same time, undermining the very different order required to undergrid sociality.

Pufendorf advanced this comprehensive system to solve the problem of 30 years of war and insecurity and to usher in an era of armed peace among states and of sociality within states. He did not foresee the flaw Montesquieu was soon to observe: the system generates a military, political and economic race that would eventually bring to ruin the life it was designed to protect (Montesquieu 1989: 13.17). The resulting insecurity of all forms of life is now the problem of the present era. As the Introduction has suggested, one way to understand this problematic state of affairs is to study the works of Pufendorf and the large role they have played in establishing the regime of political thought and action which continues to sustain it.

Bibliography

Barbeyrac, Jean, 1729   Samuel Pufendorf, *On the law of nature and nations*, 4th edition, tr. Basil Kennet, notes and 'Historical and critical account of the science of morality' by Jean Barbeyrac (London)

1820   Samuel Pufendorf, *Les Devoirs de l'homme et du citoyen tel qu'ils sont prescripts par la loi naturelle*, tr. Jean Barbeyrac, with 'le jugement de Leibnitz' (Paris: Janet et Cotelle)

Beckmann, Nicolaus and Josua Schwartz [*Index of certain novelties which Herr Samuel Pufendorf in his book On the law of nature and nations published at Lund against orthodox principles, 1673*], *Index quarundam novitatum quas dnus Samuel Puffendorff libro suo De iure naturali et gentium contra orthodoxa fundamenta Londini edidit* (Griessen)

Carmichael, Gershom, 1985   *On Samuel Pufendorf's De officio hominis et civis juxta legem naturalem libri duo* (1769), ed. John N. Lenhart, tr. Charles H. Reeves (Cleveland: Case Western Reserve University Printing Department)

Cudworth, Ralph, 1731   *Treatise concerning eternal and immutable morality*, 1731 (New York: Garland Press, 1976)

Denzer, Horst, 1972   *Moralphilosophie und Naturrecht bei Samuel Pufendorf* (Munich: C.H. Beck)

1976   *Samuel Pufendorf Die Verfassung des deutschen Reiches*, tr. with notes by Horst Denzer (Stuttgart: Reclam)

Derathé, R., 1970   *Jean-Jacques Rousseau et la science politique de son temps*, 2nd edition (Paris: J. Vrin)

Döring, Detlef, 1988   'Samuel Pufendorf (1632–1694) und die Leipziger Gelehrtengesellschaften in der mitte des 17. Jahrhunderts', *Lias*, 15, 1, pp. 13–48.

Dreitzel, Horst, 1971   'Das deutsche Staatsdenken in der frühen Neuzeit', *Neue Politische Literatur*, 16, pp. 256–71

Goyard-Fabre, Simone, 1989   'Pufendorf, adversaire de Hobbes', *Hobbes Studies*, 2, pp. 65–86.

Grotius, Hugo, 1925   *De jure belli ac pacis libri tres 1646 [1625]*, Volume 1 and *On the laws of war and peace*, Volume 2, tr. F. W. Kelsey, A. E. R.

Bibliography

Boak, H. A. Sanders and J. S. Reeves, *Classics in international law* (Oxford: Clarendon Press)

Haakonssen, Knud, 1981 *The science of a legislator: the natural jurisprudence of David Hume and Adam Smith* (Cambridge: Cambridge University Press)

1985 'Hugo Grotius and the history of political thought', *Political Theory*, 13, pp. 239–65

1991 'Natural law', in *Garland encyclopedia of ethics*, ed. Lawrence C. Becker (New York: Garland)

Hobbes, Thomas, 1983 [*Of the citizen*], *De cive: the English version* (Oxford: Clarendon Press)

Hont, Istvan, 1987 'The language of sociability and commerce: Samuel Pufendorf and the theoretical foundations of the "four stages" theory', in *The languages of political theory in early-modern Europe*, ed. Anthony Pagden (Cambridge: Cambridge University Press), pp. 253–76

1989 'Unsocial sociability and the eighteenth-century discourse of politics and society: natural law, political economy, and histories of mankind', written for The Workshop on Modern Natural Law, convened by Istvan Hont and Hans Erich Bodeker, Max Planck Institute for History, Göttingen, Germany (26–30 June 1989)

Laurent, Pierre, 1982 *Pufendorf et la loi naturelle* (Paris: J. Vrin)

Lee, Henry, 1702 *Anti-scepticism* (London)

Leibniz, Gottfried Wilhelm, 1677 'Caesarini Furstenerii de jure suprematus ac legationis principum Germaniae', in Leibniz, *Sämtliche Schriften und Briefe*, Reihe 4, Bd. 2 (Berlin: Akademie Verlag, 1963), pp. 3–270; partly tr. in Leibniz, *Political writings*, ed. Patrick Riley (Cambridge: Cambridge University Press, 1988), pp. 111–21.

1698 'On nature itself', in *Philosophical essays*, tr. Roger Ariew and Daniel Garber (Indianapolis: Hackett Publishing Company, 1989), pp. 155–66

1706 'Opinion on the principles of Pufendorf', in Leibniz, *Political writings*, ed. Patrick Riley, pp. 64–76

Loemker, Leroy, 1972 *Struggle for synthesis: the seventeenth century background of Leibniz's synthesis of order and freedom* (Cambridge, MA: Harvard University Press)

McNeill, William H., 1982 *The pursuit of power: technology, armed force, and society since A.D. 1000* (Chicago: The University of Chicago Press)

Medick, Hans, 1973 *Naturzustand und Naturgeschichte der burgerlichen Gesellschaft: die Ursprunge der burgerlichen Sozialtheorie als Geschichtsphilosophie und Sozialwissenschaft bei Samuel Pufendorf, John Locke und Adam Smith* (Göttingen: Vandenhoeck und Ruprecht)

Mellor, Anne K., 1989 *Mary Shelley: her life, her fiction, her monsters* (New York: Routledge)

Montesquieu, Charles-Louis de Secondat, 1989 *The spirit of the laws*, ed. Anne M. Cohler, Basia Carolyn Miller and Harold S. Stone (Cambridge: Cambridge University Press)

Moore, James, and Michael Silverthorne, 1983 'Natural sociability and natural rights in the moral philosophy of Gershom Carmichael', in *Philosophers of the Scottish Enlightenment* (Edinburgh: Edinburgh University Press), pp. 1–12

1989 'Natural law and fallen human nature: the reformed jurisprudence of Ulrich Huber and Gershom Carmichael', written for The Workshop on Modern Natural Law, convened by Istvan Hont and Hans Erich Bodeker, Max Planck Institute for History, Göttingen, Germany (26–30 June 1989)

Palladini, Fiammetta, 1978 *Discussioni seicentesche su Samuel Pufendorf scritti latini: 1663–1700* (Bologna; Il Mulino, Centro di Studio per la Storia della Storiografia Filosofica)

1989 'Is the "socialitas" of Pufendorf really anti-Hobbesian?', written for The Workshop on Modern Natural Law, convened by Istvan Hont and Hans Erich Bodeker, Max Planck Institute for History, Göttingen, Germany (26–30 June 1989)

Pufendorf discepolo di Hobbes (forthcoming)

Pocock, J. G. A., 1985 'Virtues, rights, and manners: a model for historians of political thought', in *Virtue, commerce, and history* (Cambridge: Cambridge University Press), pp. 37–50

Pufendorf, Samuel, 1934 *De iure naturae et gentium libri octo, 1688*, Volume 1, and *On the law of nature and nations*, Volume 2, tr. C. H. and W. A. Oldfather, *Classics of international law* (Oxford: Clarendon Press)

1716 *De iure naturae et gentium, cum annotatis Joannis Nicolai Hertii* (Frankfurt am Main). Contains *ES*

Schneewind, J. B., 1987 'Pufendorf's place in the history of ethics', *Synthese*, 72, pp. 123–55.

Seidler, Michael, 1990 *Samuel Pufendorf's 'On the natural state of men'*, the 1678 Latin edition and English translation (Lewiston, NY: The Edwin Mellon Press)

Seneca, Lucius Annaeus, 1972 *De beneficiis. Des bienfaits*, 2 vols., text established and tr. François Perchac (Paris: Belles Lettres)

Shelley, Mary, 1818 *Frankenstein or the modern Prometheus* (London: Lackington, Hughes, Harding, Mavor and Jones)

Skinner, Quentin, 1989 'The state', in *Political innovation and conceptual change*, ed. Terence Ball, James Farr and Russell Hanson (New York: Cambridge University Press), pp. 90–131.

Taylor, Charles, 1989 *Sources of the self: the making of the modern identity* (Cambridge, MA: Harvard University Press)

Tuck, Richard, 1987 'The "modern" theory of natural law', in *The languages of political theory in early-modern Europe*, ed. Anthony Pagden (Cambridge: Cambridge University Press), pp. 99–122

Tully, James, 1988 'Governing conduct', in *Conscience and casuistry in early modern Europe*, ed. Edmund Leites (Cambridge: Cambridge University Press), pp. 12–71

Williams, Bernard, 1985 *Ethics and the limits of philosophy* (Cambridge, MA: Harvard University Press)

Zurbuchen, Simone, 1986 'Naturrecht und natürliche Religion bei Samuel Pufendorf', *Studia philosophica* (Switzerland), 45, pp. 176–86

Bibliographical note

The most comprehensive bibliography of the publication of Pufendorf's works is in Denzer 1972. A photographic reprint of the 1686 Latin edition of *DJN* and an English translation by C. W. and W. A. Oldfather are available in the *Classics of international law* series ed. James Brown Scott, Carnegie Foundation for International Peace (no. 17, Oxford and New York, 1934). Latin and English editions of *EJU* and *DOH* are also available in this series (nos. 15 and 10). The 1729 and 1749 English editions of *DJN* translated by Basil Kennet include Jean Barbeyrac's useful notes and Carew's translation of Barbeyrac's 'A historical and critical account of the science of morality' from his French translation of *DJN* (1706). *ES* is available in the 1716 edition of *DJN* ed. J. Hertius and in the 1744 and 1759 editions ed. Moscovius. Many of Pufendorf's works are available in microform series, either in their original language or in English translation, such as *Early English books 1641–1700*.

For a general introduction the best place to start is Seidler's 'introductory essay' to his edition and translation of Pufendorf's 'On the natural state of men' (Seidler 1990). This includes a fine analysis of Pufendorf's concept of the state of nature, an introduction to seventeenth-century natural law philosophy, a short biography of Pufendorf, a survey of twentieth-century interpretations of Pufendorf's philosophy, and a comprehensive bibliography of secondary studies. Leonard Krieger, *The politics of discretion: Pufendorf and the acceptance of natural law* (Chicago: University of Chicago Press, 1969), the only full-length study in English, is a solid introduction to Pufendorf's life and political thought. Denzer 1972 is a classic study of Pufendorf's moral and political philosophy. A very useful summary of the major criticisms of Pufendorf to 1700 is given by Palladini 1978. Haakonssen 1991 is a concise introduction to natural law philosophy in general. For an extensive study of Pufendorf on natural law, see Laurent 1982. Schneewind 1987 analyses Pufendorf's theory of natural law and places it in the broad history of European ethical theory. Loemker 1972, Pocock 1985, Hont 1989, and Taylor 1989 all advance views on the role of seventeenth-century theories of natural law in the formation of modern moral and political thought.

For Pufendorf's concept of rights relative to his predecessors, especially Grotius and Hobbes, see Richard Tuck, *Natural rights theories* (Cambridge: Cambridge University Press, 1979). Pufendorf's relation to Grotius and Hobbes has always been problematic. According to Tuck 1987, Pufendorf is a member of a school of modern, natural law that was founded by Grotius. Palladini (1989 and 1990) argues that Pufendorf is a disciple of Hobbes who covered over this affiliation by referring to Grotius, whereas Goyard-Fabre 1989 sees him as a critic of Hobbes and Drietzel 1971 draws attention to orthodox, Lutheran–Aristotelian themes in Pufendorf's work.

Pufendorf's influence on the Enlightenment is a major topic. Moore and Silverthorne 1983 and 1989 discuss his reception in the early Scottish Enlightenment, especially by Gershom Carmichael. See also Carmichael 1985. The relation of Pufendorf's concept of sociality to theories of commercial society is set forth by Hont 1987. For Pufendorf and Rousseau see Derathé 1970. A number of studies seek to trace Pufendorf's role in the eighteenth century to Adam Smith: Medick 1973, Haakonssen 1981, Richard F. Teichgraeber, *Free trade and moral philosophy: rethinking the sources of Adam Smith's wealth of nations* (Chapel Hill, NC: Duke University Press, 1986), and Stephen Buckle, *The natural history of property* (Oxford: Oxford University Press, 1991).

Pufendorf's concepts of the state, subjection, obedience and inter-state relations have not been studied as thoroughly as his moral theory. The classic analysis of his concept of sovereignty is Otto von Gierke, *Natural law and the theory of society 1500–1800*, tr. E. Barker, 2 vols. (Cambridge: Cambridge University Press, 1934). For the intellectual background see Skinner 1989. Samuel Nutkiewicz, 'Samuel Pufendorf: obligation as the basis of the state', *Journal of the History of*

Philosophy, 21 (1983), pp. 15–29 treats obedience. Pufendorf's concepts of regular and irregular states and his analysis of the German constitution are discussed in Denzer 1976. Marc Raeff, *The well-ordered police state* (Yale: Yale University Press, 1981) is a useful introduction to seventeenth-century state-building. Horst Rabe, *Naturrecht und Kirche bei Samuel von Pufendorf* (Cologne: Böhlau, 1958) and Zurbuchen 1986 both explicate Pufendorf's proposals for church–state relations. Pufendorf's contribution to international law is canvassed in the introduction by Walter Simon to *DJN* 1934.

The subjection of women to men, their exclusion from politics, and the effect these parts of Pufendorf's political theory have on his major concepts have received little attention. For an introduction see Jane Rendall, 'Virtue and commerce: women in the making of Adam Smith's political economy', in *Women in western political philosophy*, ed. Ellen Kennedy and Susan Mendus (New York: St Martin's Press, 1987), pp. 44–77, 46–54. As Mellor 1989 suggests, Shelley 1818 challenges the assumption underlying Pufendorf's theory and the political thought of the entire age: that men alone, with their exclusively male values and sources, are able to give 'birth' to entities such as states which civilize humanity. Rather, they create destructive monsters. Pufendorf's separation of natural law from the world of nature is treated briefly from an ecological perspective in Roderick Nash, *The rights of nature: a history of environmental ethics* (Madison: University of Wisconsin Press, 1988).

Translator's note

This translation of *De officio hominis et civis juxta legem naturalem libri duo* is made from the first edition of 1673.[1] The translator and editor would like to thank David Rees, former Fellow and Tutor in Philosophy, Jesus College, Oxford, for providing them with a copy of this edition from the Fellows' Library of Jesus College. Gershom Carmichael's edition of 1724 (see following note), a copy of which was provided by Professor James Moore, has also been consulted. Earlier translations into English by Andrew Tooke 4th edition (1716)[3] and Frank Gardner Moore (1925)[4] have sometimes provided an appropriate word or turn of phrase. The translator and editor are also grateful to Mr Leszek Wysocki of McGill University, who gave the translator the benefit of his acute sense of Latin idiom, and to two amanuenses, Mrs Faye Scrim Smith and Mr Christopher Silverthorne. Gratitude is also due to the Faculty of Graduate Studies and Research at McGill University for financial support.

[1] S. Pufendorf, *De officio hominis et civis juxta legem naturalem libri duo* (Lund, 1673). The first publication of the text by Cambridge University Press appeared in 1681.

[2] S. Pufendorf, *De officio hominis et civis juxta legem naturalem libri duo supplementis et observationibus in academicae juventutis usum auxit et illustravit Gerschomus Carmichael* (Edinburgh, 1724).

[3] *The whole duty of man according to the law of nature, by that famous civilian Samuel Pufendorf ... now made English by Andrew Tooke M.A. Professor of geometry at Gresham College* (4th edition, London, 1716).

[4] S. von Pufendorf, *The two books on the duty of man and citizen according to the natural law*, translated by Frank Gardner Moore (New York, 1925).

Samuel Pufendorf

ON THE DUTY OF MAN AND CITIZEN
ACCORDING TO NATURAL LAW

IN TWO BOOKS

[LUND (ADAM JUNGHANS) 1673]

Author's dedication

To the most illustrious and exalted hero, Lord Gustavus Otto Steenbock, Count in Bogesund, Free Baron in Chronebech and Ohresteen, etc., Chief Admiral of the Kingdom of Sweden, and Chancellor of the Caroline Academy of the Goths, etc.

Most illustrious and exalted Count, most gracious Lord,
Whether it would be quite proper to claim the auspices of so illustrious a name for so slight a work as this has been the occasion of serious scruple and anxious reflection. For I was (on the one hand) very much ashamed of the modesty of a volume which affords no opportunity for wit or brilliance, since it comprises merely the first rudiments of moral philosophy, almost wholly excerpted from our longer work. Though it may perhaps be of use to those who are taking their first steps in this subject, yet it did not appear to be consonant either with your eminence or with my obligation. On the other hand, devoted as I am to your most illustrious Excellency, I was led by your private no less than by your public services to believe that I might rightly fear to be criticized for ingratitude if I neglected any opportunity, however slight it might be, at least to declare the extent of my obligation to you.

I am not speaking of those past services by which you have rendered your country in the highest degree obliged to you for your magnificent accomplishments at home and abroad, and have at the same time long since dedicated your name to immortal glory. To recount these is the task of history, which as it labours over the glorious deeds of your nation, the successful progress of her arms through so much of the world, finds you ever foremost in so many great actions. History no less admires your proficiency in the arts of peace after you retired from military service, your appointment first to the administration of a great province and then to the defence and government of the whole kingdom. My duty, rather, is to commemorate all that has been done by your illustrious Excellency for this new academy in which, at the invitation of his Majesty the King, it has been granted to me to find a place. She cannot sufficiently proclaim as they deserve the wisdom and benevolence of your protection and presidency of her; every day she finds new instances of your tireless efforts, amid the press of public business, to benefit and adorn her.

As for the benefits which your most illustrious Excellency has conferred specifically on me, how can I give them the honour they deserve? For others the sum of their wishes is to become known by men of high rank and gain their approval. But your patronage of me has been so liberally, so graciously, bestowed that I have more than once experienced your benevolent influence both in promoting my interest and in turning aside the assaults of those who wish me ill. Though it is far beyond the limit of my fortune in any way to make repayment, yet surely the least I am obliged to do is to show evidence of a humbly respectful heart and make frank acknowledgement of so many benefits received. The kindness of great men has this quality too, that it gladly allows itself to be satisfied with the evidence of a grateful heart. And it is the way of the noble and magnanimous to enhance by their acceptance the value of the duty done even by a slight show of reverence. And therefore the goodness of your most illustrious Excellency bids me hope that I shall not be thought to have fallen short of your eminence, if I use so slender a work as the occasion of giving public expression to my great devotion towards you. It would be vain to expect from me any greater work, more splendid to resist the passage of time. Men's wits are monstrously dulled to find that, as they labour to extricate themselves from the common herd, spite and ignorance gnash their teeth at them and allow no scope for rest. Yet my mind will bloom with renewed vigour and cast off its mounting weariness if I learn that your illustrious Excellency has deigned to accept this my act of homage with favour, and if at the same time you bid me rest assured of your favour and your protection for the future.

So may the great and good God preserve your most illustrious

Excellency to wax and flourish through many years, to the glory and profit of your country, of your most noble family and of our new regime.

> To your most illustrious Excellency,
> Your devoted,
> Samuel Pufendorf

Lund
X Kal. Feb. A.
1673

Author's preface

To the benevolent reader – greetings.

It would seem superfluous, if the practice of so many learned men had not made it almost mandatory, to write a preface explaining the purpose of this work. It is immediately clear that I have done no more than expound to beginners the principal topics of natural law in a short and, I hope, lucid compendium. I would not want students to be put off at the beginning by a massive accumulation of difficult questions, as would happen if they were to set out on the wide expanses of this subject without a knowledge of what one might call the elements. I also believe it to be in the public interest to steep their minds in a moral doctrine whose usefulness in civil life is accepted as obvious. In any other case I would naturally take it to be too trivial a task to reduce an extensive work to the form of a compendium, particularly a work of my own; but I think that in this case no sensible person will blame me for spending so much labour on a task which is uniquely useful to young people, particularly as I undertook it at the behest of my superiors. One's obligation to the young is such that no work undertaken for their benefit should be thought to be below anyone's dignity even if it gives no opportunity for brilliant or profound thought. Besides, no one with even a grain of sense will deny that such basic principles are better suited to the universal discipline of law than are the elements of any particular system of civil law.

So much might have seemed sufficient, but certain people have advised me that it would be pertinent to make some remarks directed towards understanding the character of natural law in general and towards a careful delineation of its boundaries. I am the more happy to do this as I may in this way remove the excuse for men of misplaced subtlety to apply their feverish criticism to the discipline of natural law. It is quite distinct from their province; there is a line of demarcation between them.

I It is evident that there are three sources of man's knowledge of his duty, of what he is to do in this life because it is right [*honestum*] and of what he is to omit because it is wrong [*turpe*]: the light of reason, the civil laws and the particular revelation of the Divinity. From the first flow the most common duties of a man, particularly those which render him capable of society [*sociabilis*] with other men; from the second flow the duties of a man as a citizen living in a particular and definite state [*civitas*]; from the third, the duties of a Christian. Hence there are three distinct disciplines. The first is the discipline of natural law, which is common to all nations; the second is the discipline of the civil law of individual states, which has, or may have, as many forms as there are states into which the human race is divided; the third discipline is called moral theology, and is distinct from the part of theology which explains the articles of our faith.

II Each of these disciplines has its own method of proving its dogmas, corresponding to its principle. In natural law a thing is affirmed as to be done because it is inferred by right reason to be essential to sociality [*socialitas*] among men. The ultimate foundation of the precepts of civil law is that the legislator has imposed them. The final reference point of the moral theologian is that God has so commanded in the Holy Scriptures.

III The discipline of civil law presupposes natural law as the more general discipline. However if there is anything in civil law on which natural law is silent, it should not be thought for that reason that the latter contradicts the former. Similarly, if anything is taught in moral theology on the basis of divine revelation beyond the scope of our reason and therefore unknown to natural law, it would be very ignorant to set these disciplines against each other or to imagine any contradiction between them. And vice versa any positions which the discipline of natural law adopts as a result of an investigation based on reason, are not on that account in any way opposed to the more explicit teaching of the Holy Scriptures on the same subject; it is merely that they are formulated by a process of abstraction [*abstrahendo*]. For example, in the discipline of natural law, we abstract from knowledge drawn from Holy Scripture and form a conception of the condition of the first man so far as reasoning alone can achieve it, however he may have been put into the world. To set that in opposition to what the Divine Scriptures teach about that condition is the very essence of black malignity and is pure malice.[1]

It is in fact easy to show a harmonious relation between civil law and natural law but it seems to be a more arduous task to fix the boundaries between natural law and moral theology and to determine in what parts particularly they most differ. I will give my opinion of this in a few words. I do not of course speak with papal authority as if I had the privilege of being guaranteed free of error, nor as if I were inspired on the basis of dreams sent from God or by an irrational instinct relying on some extraordinary illumination. I speak simply as one whose ambition it is to adorn, as his modest talents allow, the Sparta which is allotted to him. I am prepared to welcome suggestions for improvement from intelligent and learned men, and am ready to review the positions I have taken, but by the same token I have no time at all for the critics who imitate Midas and rashly jump to conclusions about things that are not their business, or for those like the tribe of Ardeliones whose character Phaedrus hits off so wittily: 'running around in circles', as he puts it, 'busy in idleness, sweating for nothing, always doing and never done, a torment to themselves and a great nuisance to everybody else'.[2]

IV 1. The first difference, then, which distinguishes those disciplines from each other results from the different sources from which they draw their dogmas. We have already touched on this. It follows that if there is anything which we are commanded to do or not to do by the Holy Scriptures, of which reason by itself cannot see the necessity, it is beyond the scope of natural law and properly belongs to moral theology.

V 2. Besides, in theology law is seen as having a divine promise attached to it and a certain kind of covenant between God and men. Natural law abstracts from this conception, since it derives from a special revelation from God which reason alone cannot find out.

VI 3. But by far the greatest difference is that the scope of the discipline of natural law is confined within the orbit of this life, and so it forms man on the assumption that he is to lead this life in society with others [*hanc vitam cum aliis sociabilem exigere debeat*]. Moral theology,

---

[1] *Cf.* Horace, *Satires*, 1.4.100–1.   [2] Phaedrus, *Fables*, 2.5.1ff.

8

however, forms a Christian man, who, beyond his duty to pass this life in goodness, has an expectation of reward for piety in the life to come and who therefore has his citizenship [*politeuma*] in the heavens while here he lives merely as a pilgrim or stranger.[3]

The human heart does indeed yearn for immortality with a burning passion and violently rejects its own destruction, and hence many nations of the gentiles have seen the rise of a belief that the soul survives separation from the body, and that then it will be good for good men and bad for evil men; however a belief on these matters in which the human mind can fully and firmly acquiesce is drawn from the word of God alone. Hence, too, the decrees of natural law are fitted only to the human court because human jurisdiction does not go beyond this life. They are indeed sometimes applied to the court of God, but wrongly, since that is very much the domain of theology.

VII 4. From this it also follows that as human jurisdiction is concerned only with a man's external actions and does not penetrate to what is hidden in the heart and which gives no external effect or sign, and consequently takes no account of it, natural law too is largely concerned with forming men's external actions. For moral theology, however, it is not enough to mould men's external conduct to propriety. Its chief task is to conform the mind and its internal motions to the will of God; and it condemns actions which seem externally to be correct but which proceed from an impure heart. This also seems to be the reason why there is less discussion in Holy Scripture about actions which are judged and penalized in the human court than about those which in Seneca's words are 'beyond the scope of the statutes'.[4] This is very clear to those who have closely studied the precepts and virtues taught by Scripture. However, moral theology does most effectively encourage a good quality of civil life since the actual Christian virtues, too, do as much as anything to dispose men's minds to sociality. And, vice versa, if you see anyone engaged in sedition and disrupting civil life, you may safely infer that the Christian religion may be on his lips but has never penetrated to his heart.

VIII It is on this basis that the true lines of distinction between natural law as we teach it and moral theology become, in my opinion, per-

---

[3] *Cf.* the Epistle of Paul to the Philippians, 3:20.

[4] Seneca, *De ira*, 2.28.2.

fectly clear. And it also becomes clear that natural law is not at all in conflict with the dogmas of true theology; it simply abstracts from certain theological dogmas which cannot be investigated by reason alone.

Hence it is also obvious that man must now be regarded by the discipline of natural law as one whose nature has been corrupted and thus as an animal seething with evil desires. For although no one is so imperceptive as not to be aware of unruly and deviant passions in himself, still without the illumination of Holy Scripture, he could not know for certain that this rebellion of the passions came by fault of the first man. Consequently, since natural law does not extend where reason cannot reach, it would be inappropriate to try to deduce natural law from the uncorrupted nature of man. This is all the more the case since many commandments[5] of the Decalogue itself, being couched in negative terms, obviously assume that man's nature is corrupt. So, for example, the first commandment certainly seems to assume that man is prone to believe in idolatry and polytheism. Suppose there were a man endowed with a nature still uncorrupted whose knowledge of God was transparent, and who consequently enjoyed His familiar (so to speak) revelation. I do not see how it could ever come into his mind to make for himself something which he would want to worship with or instead of the true God, or to believe there was divinity in something he himself had made. So this man would have had no need of the negative injunction not to worship strange gods. The simple and affirmative precept would have been enough for him: 'thou shalt love, honour and worship God whom you know as your Creator and the Creator of the universe around you'. The same holds for the second commandment. For why would a man be forbidden by a negative precept to 'blaspheme God', if he were clearly aware of His majesty and loving kindness, not tossed about by evil desires and content to accept the position God had given him? How could he be so insane? He would only need to be reminded by an affirmative precept to give glory to the name of God. It is different, however, with the third and fourth commandments, which are affirmative, and do not necessarily presuppose a corrupt nature, and are therefore applicable in both states. But with the rest of the commandments, which have regard to one's neighbour, the thing is once again

---

[5] *Praecepta*, a word used also of the 'precepts' of natural law. For the following passage see Exodus, 20:1–17.

quite obvious. For all that you needed to tell man as he was created in the beginning by God was to love his neighbour – he was inclined to do so in any case by nature. But how could one have given him the precept not to kill, when death, which came into the world through sin, had not yet fallen upon man?[6] Now, however, we have a powerful need of the negative precept; for instead of love, so much hatred stalks about the world, that there are even great numbers of people who from sheer envy or a passion to get possession of someone else's fortune do not hesitate to ruin others who are not only innocent but also their friends and benefactors; such people are not even ashamed to exploit that phrase of pious scruple 'if God will' to promote the savage and unconsidered impulses of their turbulent spirits. And what need was there expressly to forbid adultery among spouses who embraced each other with passionate, unfeigned love? Or what was the point of forbidding thefts, when there was as yet neither greed nor poverty, and no one regarded anything as his own which could help another? Or why was it necessary to prohibit false testimony when men did not yet exist willing to win fame and glory for themselves by staining others with crude and disgusting calumnies? It would not be inappropriate to apply the words of Tacitus: 'The earliest men, when there was as yet no evil lust, lived their lives without sin and crime, and therefore without punishment and sanctions; and as they desired nothing contrary to good morals, they were forbidden nothing through fear.'[7]

A proper understanding of this may open the way to solving the following problem: would the law have been different in the state of uncorrupted nature, or would it have been the same? The short answer is that the main principles of the law are the same in both states, but many particular precepts are different because of the difference in the human condition. Or rather, the same sum of the law may be laid out in different (but not contradictory) precepts according to the different conditions in which those who must obey it live.

Our Saviour reduced the sum of the law to two principles: love God and love your neighbour.[8] The whole natural law may be derived from these principles in man's corrupt as well as in his uncorrupt state (with the proviso that in his uncorrupt state there would seem to have been little if any distinction between natural law and moral theology).

---

[6] *Cf.* the Epistle of Paul to the Romans, 5:12.   [7] Tacitus, *Annals*, 3.26.
[8] *Cf.* Matthew, 22:37–9.

For sociality too, which we have laid out as the foundation of natural law, can readily be resolved into love of one's neighbour. But when one descends to particular precepts, an important distinction naturally emerges with regard to both affirmative and negative precepts. In this our present state there are a large number of affirmative precepts which seem to have had no place in the primeval state. This is partly because they presuppose institutions which (for all that we know) did not exist in mankind's condition of felicity; and partly because they are unintelligible without poverty and death, which were foreign to that state. For example, we now have among the precepts of natural law: do not deceive anyone in buying and selling; do not use a false length, weight or measure; return borrowed money at the agreed time. But we have not yet clearly resolved the question whether, if the human race had continued without sin, we would practise the kind of commerce that we now practise, and whether there would then have been any use for money. Similarly, if states as they now exist had no place in the condition of innocence, there would also have been no room there for precepts which assume the existence of states of that kind and the power of government contained in them. We are also now bidden by natural law to help the poor, to come to the aid of those stricken by undeserved disaster and to care for widows and orphans. Yet it is irrelevant to address these precepts to those who are not liable to poverty, destitution and death. Natural law also now bids us forgive wrongs and be ready to make peace – pointless among those who do not sin against the laws of sociality.

The same thing is clearly seen too in negative precepts, which depend upon natural law (not positive law) as it now is. For although every affirmative precept implicitly contains a prohibition of its opposite, for example, he who is told to love his neighbour is by that very fact forbidden to inflict on him anything inconsistent with love, nevertheless it seems superfluous to forbid such things in explicit precepts, when no evil desires prompt one to do them. To illustrate this, one may adduce Solon's refusal to assign a punishment for parricides in the public law because he did not think any son would actually commit such a crime. This is similar to the story which Francisco Lopez de Gomara (Hist. Gen. Ind. Occident, ch. 207)[9] tells of the peoples of Nicaragua, that no penalty was laid down among

---

[9] Francisco Lopez de Gomara, *La istoria de las Indias, y conquista de Mexico* (Saragossa, 1552).

them for one who had killed a chieftain (whom they call a *cacique*), because, they said, no subject would wish to plan or perpetrate such a dreadful crime.

I fear some may think it pedantic to stress points which are so obvious to most people. But I will add one example which even the first-year students will understand. Two boys of very different character have been entrusted to someone for their education. One is modest, scrupulous and afire with the love of letters; the other is dissolute and saucy, more in love with lewd desires than with books. The sum of their duty is the same for both, to learn letters; but the particular precepts will be different. For the former it is enough to give him a schedule and plan of studies to follow. The other, however, besides this, must be admonished with the direst threats not to run around, not to gamble, not to sell his books, not to plagiarize other students' work, not to carouse, not to run after prostitutes. If anyone takes upon himself the superfluous task of giving moral advice to a boy of the former character, the boy will tell him not to speak such obscenities and to give that kind of advice to anybody but him, because he has no inclination to that kind of thing.

I think it is clear from this that the face of natural law would be quite different if it were based on the supposition that the state of man is uncorrupted. And at the same time, since the boundaries which separate natural law from moral theology are so clearly marked, this discipline is in no worse position than civil jurisprudence, medicine, natural science or mathematics. If anyone dares to break into those subjects without being initiated and assumes the right to pass judgement without the approval of the professionals, they do not hesitate to apply to him the snide remark that Apelles once made to Megabyzus, who was attempting a lecture on the art of painting: 'I beg you to shut up', he said, 'before the boys who crush the pigment start laughing at you; you are trying to talk about something you've never learned.'[10] We shall easily see eye to eye with honest men of good sense. But as for malevolent and ignorant detractors, it would be better to leave them to the torment of their own jealousy, since it is a certain truth, laid down by everlasting law, that the Ethiopian does not change his skin.[11]

[10] *Cf.* Plutarch, *Moralia*, 58D ('*Quomodo adulator ab amico internoscatur*').
[11] *Cf.* Jeremiah, 13:23.

Samuel Pufendorf

ON THE DUTY OF MAN AND CITIZEN
ACCORDING TO NATURAL LAW

BOOK I

I

On human action

1. By 'duty' [*officium*] here I mean human action in conformity with the commands of law on the ground of obligation. To explain this, one must first discuss the nature of human action and the nature of laws in general.

2. By 'human action' I do not mean any motion which has its origin in man's faculties [*facultas*] but only such as is begun and directed by the faculties which the great and good Creator has given to mankind above and beyond the animals. I mean motion initiated in the light of understanding and at the command of will.

3. It has been given to man to become acquainted with the diverse multiplicity of objects that he meets in this world, to compare them, and to form new notions about them. But he has also the ability to envisage his future actions, to set himself to achieve them, to fashion them to a specific norm and purpose, and to deduce the consequences; and he can tell whether past actions conform to rule. Moreover, human faculties are not all in constant and uniform operation; some of them are aroused by an internal impulse and after arousal are brought under control and direction. Finally, a man is not attracted to all objects indifferently; some he seeks, others he avoids. Often, too, he checks a motion despite the presence of the object of action; and he often selects one of several objects before him, rejecting the rest.

4. The faculty of comprehension and judgement is called understanding [*intellectus*]. It must be taken as certain that any adult of sound mind has natural light enough to enable him, with instruction and proper reflection, to achieve adequate comprehension of at least

the general precepts and principles which make for a good and peaceful life in this world; and to recognize their conformity with human nature. If this is not granted, at least in the court of man, men could hide all their wrongdoing behind a plea of invincible ignorance, since no one can be condemned in the court of man for violating a rule which is beyond his capacity to understand.

5. A man whose understanding is well informed on what is to be done or not done to the point that he knows how to give certain and incontrovertible reasons for his opinion, is said to have a right conscience. A man may, however, have a correct view of what is to be done or not done but be unable to ground it in arguments. He has acquired it perhaps from the general manner of life of his society, or from habit, or from the authority of superiors, and has no reason for taking a contrary view. Such a man is said to have probable conscience. Most men are guided by probable conscience; few have been given the gift of uncovering the causes of things.[1]

6. Some find that quite often in particular cases arguments suggest themselves for both sides of the case, and they lack the strength of judgement to see clearly which have greater weight. The usual term for this is doubtful conscience. The rule here is: one should suspend action so long as the judgement as to good and bad is uncertain. For a decision to act before the doubt is removed involves either a deliberate or a negligent infringement of law.

7. Often too the human understanding takes the false for true; it is then said to be in error. Error is called vincible, when one can avoid falling into it by due care and attention; invincible, when one could not avoid it even by employing all the diligence which the conduct of social life requires. Invincible error usually occurs in particular matters and rarely over the general precepts for living, at least among those who have a sincere desire to cherish the light of reason and to follow what is fitting in their lives. For the general precepts of natural law are plain, and those who make positive laws should and usually do take particular care to make the laws known to their subjects. Hence this kind of error does not arise without supine neglect. But in particular cases it is easy for error about the object and other circumstances of the action to creep in unintentionally and without fault.

8. Ignorance is simply the absence of knowledge. Two forms occur,

---

[1] '*rerum cognoscere causas*', Vergil, *Georgics*, 2.490.

which are distinguished by whether ignorance contributes anything to the action or not and whether its origin is involuntary or to some degree culpable.

In the first respect, ignorance is usually divided into efficacious ignorance and concomitant ignorance. It is efficacious if, in its absence, the action in question would not have been done; it is concomitant if the action would have been done anyway despite its absence.

In the second respect, ignorance is either voluntary or involuntary. It is voluntary ignorance when one has deliberately incurred it by ignoring the means of knowing the truth, or if one has allowed it to creep up on one by failing to show due diligence. It is involuntary ignorance when one does not know what one could not have known and was not obliged to know. The latter is itself twofold. For it may happen that one cannot now shed one's ignorance, however culpable it may have been to incur it in the first place. Or one may not be able to overcome present ignorance but not be to blame for having fallen into such a condition in the first place.

9. The other faculty which is seen to be peculiar to man as opposed to the beasts is called will. Man moves himself to action by means of the will, as by a kind of internal impulse [*velut intrinseco impulsu*], and chooses what most pleases him and rejects what seems not to suit him. Man owes to his will two things: first, that he acts of his own accord, that is, he is not determined to act by some internal necessity but is himself the author of his own action; second, that he acts freely, that is, when an object is set before him, he can act or not act, he can choose or reject it, or he can choose one of several objects set before him and reject the rest.

Some human actions are done for themselves, others because they help towards the achievement of something else; that is, some have the character of an end, others of a means. In the case of an end, the will is involved in the following way: it first approves of it when it is known, then sets itself effectively into motion to attain it, and strives, so to speak, towards it either with vigour or in a gentler fashion. On obtaining its end, it comes to rest and quietly enjoys it. Means, on the other hand, are first inspected, then those which are judged most appropriate are selected and finally put into action.

10. It is particularly because a man engages in his actions voluntarily that he is held to be the author of them; in the same way, the first

point to be noted about the will is that its spontaneity [*spontaneitas*] must be asserted without fail, at least in respect to those actions for which a person is normally held to account in the court of man. But where he has no spontaneity left to him at all, it is not the man himself but the one who put compulsion on him who will be held to be the author of the action to which the other unwillingly lends his limbs and strength.

11. Although the will always seeks good in general and avoids evil in general, yet one finds in individuals a great variety of appetites and actions. This comes from the fact that all goods and evils do not appear to a man in what one may call a pure state, but mingled together, good with evil, evil with good. And different objects particularly affect what one might call different parts of a man. For example, some affect the value which he puts on himself, some his external senses, some the self-love by which he seeks his own preservation. It is for this reason that a man perceives the first class as fitting [*decora*], the second as pleasant [*jucunda*], the third as useful [*utilia*]. Each of these draws a man towards itself, in accordance with the strength of the motion which it impresses on him. Moreover, most people have a particular inclination towards certain things and an aversion from others. And so it comes about, in regard to almost any action at all, that appearances of good and evil, of the true and the plausible, offer themselves at one and the same time, and people vary in their shrewdness and ability to tell them apart. It is no wonder then that one man is attracted to what another turns away from in horror.

12. But a man's will is not observed to be always as it were poised in equilibrium on the brink of every action in such a way that its inclination in this or that direction proceeds from an impulse internal to itself after mature reflection on all points. Very often a man is tipped in one direction rather than another by what one might call external influences [*momenta*]. We will pass over men's common proclivity to evil; this is not the place to expatiate on its origin and character. But in the first place, the particular disposition of a mind communicates a certain inclination to the will, by which some are rendered liable to a certain kind of action. This is seen not only in individuals but in whole nations. It seems to be produced by the character of the climate and of the earth, by the blending of humours in the body which arises from the seed itself, from age, food, state of health, way of life and like causes; as also by the conformation of the organs which the mind uses

to perform its functions, and so on. Here we should note that if he takes the trouble, a man can, with due care, do a good deal to blunt the edge of his temperament and alter it; furthermore, that however much force may be attributed to it, one should not accept in the human court that it is powerful enough to compel him to violate the natural law, for human judgement pays no attention to evil desires which stop short of external action. And so however obstinately nature reasserts itself (though 'expelled by the fork'),[2] it can be prevented from producing vicious external actions. The difficulty of overcoming an inclination of that kind is outweighed by the splendour of the praise that awaits the victor in this contest. But if pressures of that kind so shake the mind that nothing can repress them and prevent them from bursting out, there is still a way for the pressure to be released, so to speak, without sin.

13. Frequent repetition of actions of the same kind very much inclines the will towards them; and develops a tendency which is called habit [*consuetudo*]. The effect of habit is that a certain action is done gladly and easily, so that in the object's presence the mind seems to be as it were drawn towards it; and strongly regrets its absence. But one must note that there seems to be no habit which a man cannot cast off again if he puts his mind to it; and similarly no habit can distort a mind to the point that a man is not equal to curbing here and now at least the external acts towards which the habit inclines him. And because it was in the man's power to contract or not contract a habit of that kind, it follows that, however much habit facilitates action, nothing is lost of the value of good actions, nor is the badness of evil actions diminished. In fact a good habit in a man enhances approval, a bad habit disgrace.

14. There is an immense distance between a mind at rest in quiet and tranquillity and a mind shaken by the peculiar motions which we call passions [*affectus*]. The rule for passions is: however strong they may be, a man can rise superior to them by the due use of reason and at least check them in their course before they issue in action.

Some passions are excited by an appearance [*species*] of something good, others by an appearance of something bad; they prompt us either to get a pleasing thing or to avoid an offensive thing. It is in accord with human nature that more goodwill or indulgence should

---

[2] Horace, *Epistles*, 1.10.24.

be given to the latter passions than to the former, and all the more so the more dangerous and unendurable was the evil which aroused them. It is thought to be far easier to go without something good which is not absolutely essential to the preservation of our nature than to submit to an evil which threatens its destruction.

15. Finally, by analogy with certain illnesses which completely take away the use of reason permanently or temporarily, there is a common practice among some peoples of inflicting on themselves a kind of temporary illness which severely interferes with the use of reason. We refer to the intoxication brought on by certain kinds of substances which people drink or smoke. These substances set up a violent motion in the blood and spirits which disorders and confuses them, and makes men prone to lust (above all) and anger, recklessness and immoderate mirth. Some men seem to be beside themselves, so to speak, with intoxication, and to put on an altogether different character from the one they have when sober. Intoxication does not always wholly incapacitate the use of reason, but as it is self-inflicted, it is apt to bring actions done under its influence into disfavour rather than favour.

16. Just as human actions are called voluntary insofar as they proceed from and are directed by the will, so actions which are knowingly undertaken in opposition to the will are called involuntary, taking this word in its narrower sense; for in a broader sense it also includes actions committed through ignorance. Here then 'involuntary' means the same as 'compelled', that is, when someone is constrained to move his limbs by a more powerful external principle provided that he gives evidence of his unwillingness and lack of consent by whatever signs he can but especially by physically struggling. 'Involuntary' is also applied, less properly, to situations where under the constraint of severe necessity something is chosen (and done) as the lesser evil from which in other circumstances, without the constraint of compulsion, one would have turned away in horror. Such actions are normally called mixed. They have this in common with spontaneous actions, that the will undoubtedly selects them as the lesser evil in the actual conditions; but as far as effect is concerned, they have something in common with involuntary actions, for it is usual either not to hold the agent responsible for them at all or to attribute to him less responsibility than in the case of spontaneous actions.

17. The particular characteristic of human actions initiated and

directed by intellect and will, is that they may be imputed to a man, or that he may rightly be regarded as their author and obliged to account for them; and that their effects also redound to him. For there is no better reason why an action may be imputed to someone than that it originated with him, directly or indirectly, and that he was aware of it and willed it, or that it was in his power whether it would be done or not. Hence the primary axiom in moral disciplines which look at the subject from the point of view of the human court is held to be: a man may be held accountable for those actions which it is in his power whether they are to be done or not. It comes to the same thing to say: any action which can be under human control and whose commission or non-commission is in his power may be imputed to him. Conversely, no one may be held to be the author of an action which was not in his power either in itself or in its cause.

18. From these premises we shall form some particular propositions which will define what may be imputed to each man or what actions and events each may be held to be the author of.

First, no actions done by others, no operation of any other things and no event can be imputed to a person except insofar as he can control them and is obliged to do so. For nothing is more common among men than that a person have the responsibility of directing another person's actions. In this case if an action is done by the one party and the other party failed to do what it was in his power to do, that action will be imputed not only to the immediate doer but also to the person who failed to exercise proper direction so far as possible. However, this requirement has its limits and bounds, so that 'possible' is to be taken in the sense of moral possibility and with some reservation. For the liberty of the subjected person is not abolished by the subjection of one person to another; he may still resist the other's control and go his own way; and the conditions of human life do not allow one to monitor all of the other's movements as if he were permanently attached to him. Consequently, if the person in charge has done everything that the nature of the charge laid on him permitted, and still the other person does something wrong, it will be imputed to the doer alone.

Similarly, now that men have ownership of the animals, whenever an animal's action causes loss to a person, the owner will be held responsible if he has fallen short of the proper standard of care and custody.

Similarly a person may be held responsible for the misfortunes of others if he did not do what he could and what he should to remove their cause and occasion. For example, since men have it in their power to promote or suspend the operations of many things in nature, they will be held responsible for any advantage or loss, so far as their effort or neglect significantly contributed to the result.

Sometimes too, extraordinarily, a person is held responsible for events which are normally beyond human control, as when the deity has made a special disposition for a certain person.

Apart from these and similar cases, it is enough to be able to account for one's own actions.

19. Second, there are personal defects which it is not in a man's power to acquire or not to acquire. He cannot be held responsible for these except insofar as he did not take pains to make up a natural defect or to supplement the native powers which he does have. For example, no one can give himself a keen mind or a strong body and therefore no one can be held responsible on this score except so far as he has or has not neglected to develop these powers. So too it is not the rustic but the town-dweller and the courtier who are censured for bad manners. So it has to be seen as absolutely absurd to criticize people for qualities which are not in our power, such as being short, having a bad figure and so on.

20. Third, one cannot be held responsible for actions done through invincible ignorance. For we cannot direct an action when the light of understanding does not show the way, assuming that the man could not get such a light for himself and it was not his fault that he could not do so. Moreover in social life 'can' is understood in a moral sense as the degree of capacity, cleverness and caution which is commonly judged sufficient and which rests on probable reasons.

21. Fourth, neither ignorance nor mistake about the laws and the duty laid on us releases us from responsibility. For he who makes the laws and lays duties upon us should, and normally does, ensure that they are brought to the attention of the subject. And the laws and the rules of duty should be, and normally are, suited to the subject's understanding; and everyone should take pains to get to know them and remember them. Hence he who is a cause of ignorance will be obliged to answer for the actions which result from that ignorance.

22. Fifth, if by no fault of his own a man does not have the opportunity to act, he is not held responsible for not acting. Opportunity seems

to include four elements: (1) that the object of the action is at hand; (2) that there is a convenient place available where we cannot be impeded by others or in some way harmed; (3) that a suitable time is available at which we do not have more pressing business to attend to, and likewise that the time is good for others involved in the action; and finally, (4) that our natural powers of action are adequate. Since action is impossible without these conditions, it would actually be absurd to hold that a person has the responsibility to do something which he has no opportunity to do. For example, a doctor cannot be accused of idleness if no one is sick; a poor man has no opportunity to be generous; a man who has been refused a post for which he properly applied cannot be accused of hiding his talent; and to whom much has been given, of him much will be required;[3] we cannot suck and blow at the same time.[4]

23. Sixth, a person cannot be held responsible for not doing what exceeds his powers, and which he is unable with those powers to bring about. Hence the common phrase: there is no obligation to do the impossible. However, one must add the proviso that he not have weakened or destroyed his power to act by his own fault. For this case can be treated in the same way as if he still had his powers, since otherwise there would be an easy way of avoiding even the slightest obligation by deliberately spoiling one's power to act.

24. Seventh, a person cannot be held responsible for what he does or suffers under compulsion, assuming that avoidance or escape were beyond his powers. We may be said to be compelled in two ways: (1) when a stronger party uses force to make our limbs do or suffer something; (2) if a more powerful person threatens us at close quarters with some serious harm (and has the ability to carry out his threat right away) if we do not make a move to do something or abstain from doing it. For in this case, unless we are expressly obliged to redeem by our suffering what should be inflicted on another, it is he who lays this necessity upon us who will be taken as the originator of the crime; and we can no more be held responsible for that act than a sword or an axe for a killing.

25. Eighth, those who do not have the use of reason are not held responsible for their actions. For they are unable to discern clearly what is to be done and to compare it against a rule. This is the case

---

[3] *Cf.* Luke, 12:48.   [4] *Cf.* Plautus, *Mostellaria*, 791.

with actions of infants before the use of reason begins to show itself with any degree of clarity. Scolding or smacking children for something they have done is not intended as if (in human justice) they have deserved punishment properly so called, but purely as a means of correction and discipline, so that they will not be a nuisance to others by such behaviour or develop bad habits. Similarly in the case of the insane, the mentally disturbed and the senile, their actions are not regarded as human, since their illness arose through no fault of their own.

26. Ninth (and finally), a person cannot be held responsible for what he imagines he is doing in dreams, except insofar as by dwelling with pleasure on such things during the day he allows images of them to make a deep impression on his mind. But not much attention is usually paid to them in human judgement. For in other ways, too, imagination [*phantasia*] in sleep is like a boat adrift without a helmsman, so that it is not in a man's power to control what kind of fancies it will produce.

27. In discussing responsibility for another person's actions we must be quite clear that it sometimes happens that an action is not imputed to the actual doer at all, but to another person who used him merely as an instrument. It is more usual, however, for the action to be the joint responsibility of the doer and of the other person who contributes to it by action or omission. There are three major forms of this. Either the other person is held to be the principal cause of the action and the doer the secondary cause; or both are equally responsible; or the other person is the secondary and the doer is the principal cause.

Into the first category fall those who incited the other person to action by their own authority; those who gave the necessary consent without which the other person would not have acted; those who could and should have prevented it and did not do so.

Into the second category fall those who commission or hire someone to commit a crime; those who aid and abet; those who provide refuge and protection; those who when they could and should have offered help to the victim, did not do so.

Into the third category one may put those who give special advice; those who give assent and approval to a crime before it is done; those who encourage wrongdoing by the examples they give, and the like.

2

On the rule of human actions, or on law in general

1. Human actions arise from the will. But the acts of will of an individual are not consistent in themselves; and the wills of different men tend in different directions. For mankind to have achieved order and decency therefore, there must have been some rule to which those wills might conform. For otherwise if each man, amid so much liberty to will and such diversity of inclinations and desires, had done whatever came into his mind without reflective reference to a fixed rule, the result would inevitably have been great confusion among men.

2. This rule is called law [*lex*]. Law is a decree by which a superior obliges one who is subject to him to conform his actions to the superior's prescript [*praescriptum*].

3. To understand this definition better, one must answer these questions: what is obligation? what is its origin? who can incur obligation, and who can impose obligation on another?

Obligation is commonly defined as a bond of right by which we are constrained by the necessity of making some performance. That is, obligation places a kind of bridle on our liberty, so that, though the will can in fact take different directions it yet finds itself imbued by it with an internal sense (so to speak), so that it is compelled to recognize that it has not acted rightly if the subsequent action does not conform to the prescribed rule. Consequently, if anything bad happens to a man for that reason, he judges that he deserves it, since he could have avoided it by following the rule, as he should have done.

4. There are two reasons why man is fit to incur obligation: (1) he has a will capable of moving in various directions and so able to conform

27

to the rule; and (2) he is not free from the authority of a superior. For there is no expectation of free action where an agent's powers are tied by nature to a uniform mode of behaviour; and it is pointless to prescribe a rule to one who can neither understand nor conform to it. It follows therefore that one is capable of obligation if he has a superior, if he can recognize a prescribed rule and if he has a will which is capable of taking different directions, yet (when a rule has been prescribed by a superior) is imbued with the sense that it may not rightly deviate from it. With such a nature, it is evident, man is endowed.

5. An obligation is introduced into a man's mind by a superior, by one who has not only the strength to inflict some injury on the recalcitrant, but also just cause to require us to curtail the liberty of our will at his discretion. When a person in this position has signified his will, fear tempered by respect [*reverentia*] must arise in a man's mind [*animus*] – fear from power, respect from reflection on the reasons which ought to induce one to accept his will even apart from fear. For anyone who can give no reason except mere strength why he will impose an obligation upon me against my will can indeed terrify me, so that I think it better [*satius*] to obey him for the time being to avoid a greater evil, but when the threat is gone, nothing any longer prevents me from acting at my discretion rather than his. On the other hand, if a person has reasons why I should obey him but lacks the strength to inflict injury on me, I can disregard his orders with impunity, unless one more powerful than he comes to assert the authority I have flouted.

The reasons which justify a person's claim to another's obedience are: if he has conferred exceptional benefits on him; if it is evident that he wishes the other well and can look out for him better than he can for himself; if at the same time he actually claims direction of him; and, finally, if the other party has voluntarily submitted to him and accepted his direction.

6. For the law to exert its force in the minds to whom it applies, there must be knowledge of who the legislator is and of what the law itself is. For no one will offer obedience not knowing whom he should obey or what he is obliged to do.

It is very easy to know the legislator. For natural laws, it is clear by the light of reason that their author is the author of the universe. And as for the citizen, he cannot fail to know who has authority over him.

How natural laws become known will be explained presently. Civil laws reach subjects' notice by promulgation plainly and openly made. In promulgating a law one should make two things particularly clear: first, that the author of the law is he who holds sovereign power in the state, and secondly, what is the meaning of the law. The first point is made clear when the sovereign promulgates it with his own voice or by attaching his signature to it, or by having his delegates do these things for him. It will be in vain to call in question their authority, if it is clear that this is a function of the office they hold in the state and that they are regularly employed for this purpose; if those laws are applied in the courts; and if they contain nothing that derogates from the sovereign power. For the meaning of the law to be correctly grasped, those who promulgate it have a duty to be as perspicuous as possible. If anything obscure does turn up in the laws, a clarification must be sought from the legislator or from those who have been publicly appointed to render judgement in accordance with the laws.

7. Every complete law has two parts: the one part in which what is to be done or not done is defined, and the other which declares the punishment prescribed for one who ignores a precept or does what is forbidden. For because of the wickedness of human nature which loves to do what is forbidden, it is utterly useless to say 'Do this!' if no evil awaits him who does not, and similarly, it is absurd to say, 'You will be punished', without first specifying what deserves the punishment.

So then the whole force of the law consists in making known what the superior wants us to do or not to do and the penalty set for violators. The power of creating an obligation, that is, of imposing an internal necessity, and the power to compel or to enforce observance of the laws by means of penalties, lie properly with the legislator and with him to whom the protection and execution of the laws is committed.

8. A duty imposed on someone by law should be not only within his power but also of some use to him or to others. On the one hand, it is absurd and cruel to attempt to require something of someone under threat of penalty, if it is and always has been beyond his powers. Likewise, it is unnecessary to curtail the natural liberty of the will if no use is to come of it for anyone.

9. Although a law normally embraces all the subjects of the legislator to whom the substance of the law applies, and whom the legislator did

not specifically exempt, nevertheless it sometimes happens that a particular person may be specially exempted from the obligation of a law. This is called 'dispensation'. The power of granting a dispensation belongs only to him who has the authority to make and unmake laws. One must be careful that one does not, by indiscriminate granting of dispensations, without serious cause, undermine the authority of the laws and give an opening to envy and indignation among the subjects.

10. Equity is very different from dispensation. It is a correction of the law where law is deficient through its universality; or a skilful interpretation of the law by which it is shown from natural reason that some particular case is not covered by a general law since an absurd situation would result if it were. Not all cases can be foreseen or expressly provided for because of their infinite variety. Hence judges, who have the task of applying the general provisions of a law to particular cases, must except from the law the sort of cases that the legislator would have excepted if he had been present or if he had foreseen such cases.

11. From their relation to and congruence with a moral rule human actions acquire certain qualities and denominations.

Those actions for which the law makes no provision in either way are said to be licit or permitted. One must admit however that sometimes in civil life, where not every detail can be exactly as it should be, some things are said to be licit because they are not penalized in human courts, though in themselves they are repugnant to natural goodness.

Actions in accordance with law are called good [*bonus*]; contrary to law bad [*malus*]. For an action to be good, it must be totally in accordance with law; for an action to be bad, it need only be deficient at a single point.

12. Justice is sometimes an attribute of actions, sometimes of persons. When justice is ascribed to a person, it is usually defined as a constant and unremitting will to render to each his own.[1] The just man is defined as one who delights in doing just actions or strives after justice or attempts in everything to do what is just. The unjust man, by contrast, is he who neglects to render each his own, or who thinks that the criterion should be not his duty but his own immediate

---

[1] *Cf.* Justinian, *Institutes*, 1.1 pr., *Digest*, 1.1.10.

advantage. Consequently some of a just man's actions may be unjust and vice versa. For the just man does justice because of the law's command and injustice only through weakness; whereas the unjust man does justice because of the penalty attached to the law and injustice through the wickedness of his heart.

13. Justice as an attribute of actions is simply the appropriate fitting of actions to persons. And a just action is one which is done to the person to whom it is appropriate to do it by deliberate choice or with knowledge and intention. Thus the major difference in the case of actions between justice and goodness is that goodness denotes merely conformity with the law whereas justice involves in addition a relationship to those in respect of whom the action is done. This is also the reason why justice is said to be a virtue in respect of another person.

14. There is no agreement on the divisions of justice. The most widely accepted is the division into universal and particular. Universal justice is said to be doing duties of any kind to other people, even such duties as could not be claimed by force or by launching an action in the courts. Particular justice is doing to another precisely those things which he could have demanded of right; it is usually subdivided into distributive and commutative. Distributive justice rests on an agreement between society and its members about pro rata sharing in loss and gain. Commutative justice, by contrast, rests on a bilateral contract particularly concerned with things and actions relevant to commerce.

15. Now that we know what justice is, we can easily infer the nature of injustice. We must notice that the kind of unjust action which is done by deliberate design and which violates what is due to another by perfect right or which he possesses by perfect right (no matter how obtained), is properly called a wrong. There are three kinds of wrong: if a person is denied what he might demand in his own right (not due, that is, merely on the basis of humanity or a similar virtue); or if he is deprived of what he held in his own right, a right valid against the depriver; or if an injury is inflicted on another which we do not have the authority to inflict. Wrong also requires deliberate design and malice on the part of the agent. In the absence of malice, an injury to another is called an accident or fault [*culpa*], and the gravity or mildness of the fault depends upon the degree of carelessness or negligence which was the cause of the damage to the other party.

16. With respect to its author, law is divided into divine and human; the one was made by God, the other by man. But if it is viewed in the light of whether it has, or has not, a necessary and universal congruence with men, it is divided into natural and positive. Natural law is law which is so congruent with the rational and social nature of man that there cannot be a good and peaceful society for the human race without it. Hence too it can be traced out and known by the light of man's native reason and by reflection on human nature in general. Positive law is law which does not derive from the common condition of human nature, but proceeds solely from the will of the legislator, although it ought not to be without its own rationale and usefulness which it creates for certain men or for a particular society.

Of divine law, one kind is natural, the other positive. But all human law, strictly so called, is positive.

3
On natural law

1. What is the character of natural law? What is its necessity? And in what precepts does it consist in the actual condition of mankind? These questions are most clearly answered by a close scrutiny of the nature and character of man. Just as one makes great progress towards an accurate knowledge of civil laws by first achieving a good understanding of the condition of a state and the customs and occupations of its citizens, so if one first takes a view of the common character and condition of mankind, the laws on which man's security rests will easily become clear.

2. In common with all living things which have a sense of themselves, man holds nothing more dear than himself, he studies in every way to preserve himself, he strives to acquire what seems good to him and to repel what seems bad to him. This passion is usually so strong that all other passions give way before it. And if anyone attempts to attack a man's safety, he cannot fail to repel him, and to repel him so vigorously that hatred and desire for revenge usually last long after he has beaten off the attack.

3. On the other hand man now seems to be in a worse condition than the beasts in that scarcely any other animal is attended from birth with such weakness [*imbecillitas*]. It would be something of a miracle, if he came through to maturity without the help of other men, since even now when so many things have been discovered to relieve men's needs, a careful training of several years is required to enable a person to get his food and clothing by his own efforts. Let us imagine a man coming to adult years without any care and fostering from other men. He would have no knowledge except what has sprung by a kind of

33

spontaneous generation from his own intelligence. He would be in solitude, destitute of all the help and company of others. Evidently, one will scarcely find a more miserable animal, without speech presumably and naked, who has no resource but to tear at grass and roots or to pick wild fruits, to slake his thirst at the spring or river or from the puddle in his path, to seek shelter in caves from the assaults of the storm or to protect his body as best he may with moss or grass. Time would pass most tediously with nothing to do; at every noise or approach of another animal he would start in terror; and would at last die of hunger or cold or in the jaws of a wild beast.

By contrast, all the advantages that attend human life today derive from men's mutual assistance. There is nothing in this world, save the great and good God Himself, from which greater advantage can come to man than from man himself.

4. But this animal which is so mutually helpful suffers from a number of vices and is endowed with a considerable capacity for harm. His vices render dealing with him risky and make great caution necessary to avoid receiving evil from him instead of good.

In the first place, he is seen to have a greater tendency to do harm than any of the beasts. For the only things by which beasts are carried away are desires for food and sex, both of which they can themselves satisfy with little effort. And when these desires are laid to rest, they are not easily stirred to anger or to harm others unless provoked. But man is an animal ready for sexual activity on any occasion and tickled by the itch of lust much more frequently than would seem necessary for the preservation of the species. His belly too wants not only to be satisfied but to be titillated, and often has an appetite for more than it can naturally digest. Nature has provided that the beasts should not need clothes; but man delights in being clothed for ostentation as well as from necessity. Many other passions and desires are found in the human race unknown to the beasts, as, greed for unnecessary possessions, avarice, desire of glory and of surpassing others, envy, rivalry and intellectual strife. It is indicative that many of the wars by which the human race is broken and bruised are waged for reasons unknown to the beasts. And all these things can and do incite men to inflict harm on each other. There is moreover in many men a kind of extraordinary petulance, a passion for insulting others, at which others cannot fail to be offended and to gird themselves to resist, however restrained their natural temper, in order to preserve and

34

protect their persons and their liberty. Sometimes too men are incited to mutual injury by want and because their actual resources are not adequate to their desires or their need.

5. Men's capacity for mutual infliction of injury is also very powerful. For though unlike the beasts they are not formidable for teeth or hooves or horns, yet the dexterity of their hands can be developed into a most effective instrument of harm, and their mental ingenuity facilitates attack by cunning and stratagem where open assault is out of the question. And so it becomes very easy to inflict death, the worst of man's natural evils.

6. Finally, one must recognize in the human race, by contrast with any individual species of animals, an extraordinary variety of minds. Animals of the same species have virtually identical inclinations, are led by similar passions and appetites. But among men there are as many humours as there are heads, and each man loves his own. Men are not all moved by one simple uniform desire, but by a multiplicity of desires variously combined. In fact, one and the same man is often observed to be different from what he had been, and to recoil in horror from what he once coveted. There is no less variety in men's occupations and habits and in their inclinations to exert their powers of mind, as may be observed nowadays in the almost unlimited kinds of life men choose. For these reasons careful regulation and control are needed to keep them from coming into conflict with each other.

7. Man, then, is an animal with an intense concern for his own preservation, needy by himself, incapable of protection without the help of his fellows, and very well fitted for the mutual provision of benefits. Equally, however, he is at the same time malicious, aggressive, easily provoked and as willing as he is able to inflict harm on others. The conclusion is: in order to be safe, it is necessary for him to be sociable; that is to join forces with men like himself and so conduct himself towards them that they are not given even a plausible excuse for harming him, but rather become willing to preserve and promote his advantages [*commoda*].

8. The laws of this sociality [*socialitas*], laws which teach one how to conduct oneself to become a useful [*commodum*] member of human society, are called natural laws.

9. On this basis it is evident that the fundamental natural law is: every man ought to do as much as he can to cultivate and preserve sociality. Since he who wills the end wills also the means which are indispens-

able to achieving that end, it follows that all that necessarily and normally makes for sociality is understood to be prescribed by natural law. All that disturbs or violates sociality is understood as forbidden.

The rest of the precepts may be said to be no more than subsumptions under this general law. Their self-evidence is borne in upon us by the natural light which is native to man.

10. Though these precepts have a clear utility, they get the force of law only upon the presuppositions that God exists and rules all things by His providence, and that He has enjoined the human race to observe as laws those dictates of reason which He has Himself promulgated by the force of the innate light.[1] For otherwise though they might be observed for their utility, like the prescriptions doctors give to regulate health, they would not be laws. Laws necessarily imply a superior, and such a superior as actually has governance of another.

11. The demonstration that God is the author of natural law rests on natural reason, provided that we confine ourselves to man's present state, disregarding the question whether his primeval condition was different and how the change came about.

Man's nature, then, is so constituted that the human race cannot be secure without social life and the human mind is seen to be capable of ideas which serve this end. It is also clear not only that the human race, like other creatures, owes its origin to God, but also that whatever its present condition, it is encompassed by the government of God's providence. It follows that God wills that a man should use for the preservation of his nature the powers within him in which he is conscious of surpassing the beasts; and that he also wills that human life be different from their lawless life. Since he cannot achieve this except by observance of natural law, it is also understood that he is obligated by God to observe it as the means which God Himself has established expressly to achieve this end, and which is not a product of man's will and changeable at his pleasure. For he who obligates one to an end is held also to have obligated one to take the means necessary to that end.

It is also a sign that social life has been imposed upon men by God's authority, that the sense of religion or fear of the Deity is not found in any other living creature; this sense does not seem to be

---

[1] '*promulgatas*': *cf.* 1.2.16 on positive legislation.

intelligible in a lawless animal. This is the origin of that quite delicate sense in men who are not wholly corrupted, which convinces them that when they sin against natural law, they offend Him who has authority over men's minds, and who is to be feared even when there is nothing to be feared from men.

12. The common phrase that law is known by nature should not be taken, it seems, as implying that there are inherent in men's minds, from the moment of birth, actual, distinct propositions about what is to be done and what avoided. It means partly that law can be explored by the light of reason, and partly that at least the common and important precepts of natural law are so plain and clear that they meet with immediate assent, and become so ingrained in our minds that they can never thereafter be wiped from them, however the impious man may strive wholly to extinguish his sense of them, to lay to rest the stirrings of his conscience. On this ground, too, it is said in the Holy Scriptures to be 'written in the hearts of men'.[2] Since we are imbued with a sense of them from childhood on by the discipline of civil life, and since we cannot remember the time when we first took them in, we think that we had a knowledge of them already in us when we were born. It is the same thing as we all experience with regard to our native language.

13. Perhaps the duties imposed on man by natural law are most conveniently divided in accordance with the objects on which those duties are to be exercised. On these lines they form three principal divisions. The first teaches, on the basis of the dictate of right reason alone, how one should behave towards God; the second towards oneself; the third towards other men. The precepts of natural law regarding others are derived primarily and directly from sociality, which we have laid down as the foundation. The duties towards God as Creator also can be deduced, indirectly, from that source, insofar as the ultimate sanction of duties towards other men comes from religion and fear of the Deity, so that a man would not even be sociable if he were not imbued with religion, and because reason alone in religion extends no further than to religion's capacity to promote the tranquillity and sociality of this life; for so far as religion procures the saving of souls, it proceeds from a particular divine

---

[2] Epistle of Paul to the Romans, 2:15.

37

revelation. The duties of a man towards himself, however, emanate from religion and sociality together. For the reason why in some matters man cannot dispose of himself at his own absolute discretion, is partly that he may be fit to worship the divinity, and partly that he may be an agreeable and useful member of human society.

4

On man's duty to God, or on natural religion

1. So far as man's duty to God can be traced out on the basis of natural reason, it has no more than two articles: first, to have right notions of God, and secondly, to conform our actions to His will. Hence natural religion consists of theoretical propositions and practical propositions.

2. Of all the notions which everyone must hold about God, the first is a settled conviction that God exists, that is, that there really is a supreme and first being on whom this universe depends. This has been most plainly demonstrated by philosophers from the subordination of causes which must find an end in some first thing, from motion, from reflection on the fabric of the universe, and by similar arguments. Claiming not to understand these arguments is no excuse for atheism. For since this conviction has been a constant possession of the whole human race, anyone who wished to overthrow it would not only have to produce a solid refutation of all the arguments which prove God's existence, but also come forward with more convincing reasons for his own position. At the same time, since the salvation of the human race has been believed hitherto to depend on this conviction, he would also have to show that atheism would be better for the human race than to maintain a sound worship of God. Since this cannot be done, we must heartily detest and severely punish the impiety of all who make any attempt whatever to shatter that conviction.

3. The second notion is that God is the Creator of this universe. For since it is self-evident that all this world did not come into existence of itself, it must have a cause and that cause is what we call God.

39

It follows from this that it is an error to prattle about nature (as people do from time to time) as the final cause of all things and all effects. For if the word 'nature' is meant to be taken as the causal efficacy and power of action which is observed in things, it surely gives evidence itself of its author, God; so far is nature's power from lending support to any argument in denial of God. If, however, by 'nature' is meant the supreme cause of all things, it is a kind of fastidious profanity to avoid the plain, accepted term, God.

It is also an error to believe that God is among the objects accessible to the senses, and particularly the stars. For in all these things their substance proves that they are not primary but derived from another.

They too have an unworthy conception of God who say that He is the soul of the world. For soul of the world, whatever it may actually be, denotes a part of the world; but how could a part of a thing have been its cause, i.e. something prior to it? If on the other hand by soul of the world is meant that first, invisible something on which the force and motion of everything depends, this is to substitute an obscure, figurative expression for a plain word.

It is also obvious from this very point that the world is not eternal. For this is incompatible with the nature of anything that has a cause. Whoever asserts that the world is eternal, denies that it has any cause and so denies God Himself.

4. The third notion is that God exercises direction over the world as a whole and over the human race. This is clearly evident from the admirable and unchanging order seen in the universe. The moral effect is the same whether one denies that God exists or denies that He has concern for human affairs, since both opinions utterly undermine all religion. For there is no reason to fear or to worship a being who however excellent He may be in Himself, is unmoved by concern for us and neither can nor will confer either good or evil upon us.

5. The fourth notion is that no attribute which involves any imperfection is compatible with God. For since He is the cause and origin of all things, it would be absurd that any creature of His could form the conception of a perfection which is not in God. Moreover, since His perfection exceeds in infinite ways the intellectual capacity of so mean a creature, it will be appropriate to use negative rather than positive terms to express His perfection. Hence one must never assign to God attributes that denote anything finite or determinate, because there

could always be found something greater than anything finite. And every determination and figure involves boundaries and circumscription. In fact, one must not even say that He is distinctly and clearly understood or conceived by our imagination, or by any faculty of our soul, for whatever we have the capacity to conceive clearly and distinctly is finite. And we do not have a full conception of God in our minds simply because we speak of Him as infinite, since 'infinite' properly speaking does not denote anything in the object, but only the incapacity of our minds, as if we were saying that we do not grasp the greatness of His essence. Hence it is not correct to say that He has parts or that He is a whole, since these are attributes of finite things; nor that He exists in a certain place, since this implies bounds and limits to His greatness; nor that He moves or is at rest, since both imply existence in space.

Thus one cannot properly attribute to God anything that denotes pain or passion, for instance, anger, repentance or pity (I say 'properly' since when such things are attributed to God in Scripture, it is done in terms of human feeling [*anthropopathos*] to represent the effect not the emotion). The same is the case with whatever implies the want or absence of any good, e.g., desire, hope, craving, sexual love. They imply a lack, hence an imperfection, since desiring, hoping and craving can only be understood as directed towards what one lacks or does not have.

Similarly in the case of intellect, will, knowledge and activities of the senses, such as sight or hearing; when these are attributed to God, they must be taken to be attributed in a mode far more sublime than that in which they exist in us. For will is rational desire, and desire presupposes absence and lack of the relevant object. Also intellect and sensation in men involve an impression made by objects on the organs of the body and powers of the soul, which is an indication of a dependent and therefore less than perfect power.

Finally, it is also inconsistent with divine perfection to say that there is more than one God. For apart from the fact that the wonderful harmony of the world argues a single governor, God would actually also be finite if there were several gods of equal power not dependent on Him. The existence of more than one infinite would involve a contradiction.

All this being so, the courses most consistent with reason in the matter of the attributes of God, are: either to use negative terms, e.g.

infinite, incomprehensible, immense, eternal, that is, lacking beginning and end; or to use superlatives, e.g. best, greatest, most powerful, most wise, etc.; or to use indefinite terms, e.g. good, just, creator, king, lord, etc., not so much with the intention of actually saying distinctly what He is as of finding some kind of expression to declare our admiration and obedience; for this is the sign of a humble mind, of a mind that offers all the honour of which it is capable.

6. The practical propositions of natural religion are partly concerned with the internal, partly with the external, worship of God.

The internal worship of God is to honour Him. Honour is a conviction that power and goodness are united in someone. The human mind should naturally conceive the highest possible reverence for God in consideration of His power and goodness.

It follows from this that one should love Him as the author and giver of every good; one should hope in Him as the one on whom all our future felicity depends; one should acquiesce in His will since of His goodness He does all things for the best, and gives us what is most for our good; one should fear Him as most powerful, to offend whom is apt to incur the greatest evil; and one should offer Him in all things the most humble obedience as Creator, lord and governor, the greatest and the best.

7. The external worship of God consists particularly in the following:

(1) To give thanks to God for all the many good things men receive from Him.

(2) To express His will by their actions as far as possible, or obey Him.

(3) To admire and celebrate His greatness.

(4) To offer prayers to Him to obtain what is good and ward off evil; for prayers are signs of hope, and hope is an acknowledgement of His goodness and power.

(5) To swear by God alone (when the occasion requires) and keep one's oath scrupulously. This is what is demanded by God's omniscience and power.

(6) To speak respectfully of God; for this is a sign of fear; and fear is a confession of power. It follows from this that we should not use the name of God rashly and in vain; for both show lack of respect. One must not swear where there is no need; for that is to swear in vain. One must not engage in curious and insolent disputes about the nature and government of God; for this is

simply to attempt to reduce God to the petty measure of our own reason.

(7) Likewise, to offer to God only what is excellent of its kind and fit to show Him honour.

(8) Likewise, to worship God not only in private but also openly and publicly in the sight of men. For to keep anything hidden is as if one is ashamed of doing it. By contrast public worship not only testifies to our devotion but also stimulates others by example.

(9) Finally, to make every effort to observe the laws of nature. For slighting the authority of God is the highest of all insults; but obedience is more acceptable than any sacrifice.

8. For it is certain that the effect of this natural religion, when understood in a precise sense and in the light of man's present condition is confined to the sphere of this life; it has no effect on winning eternal salvation. For human reason left to itself is quite ignorant that the depravity seen in man's faculties and inclinations is the result of human fault and merits God's indignation and eternal death. Hence too the need of a Saviour, the need of His work and merit, and of the promises which God has made to the human race and all that flows from that, are unknown to human reason, although it is clear from Holy Scripture that these are the only means by which eternal salvation comes to man.

9. It would further be worthwhile to weigh up a little more distinctly the usefulness of religion in human life, to establish that it really is the ultimate and the strongest bond of human society.

For in natural liberty, if you do away with fear of the Deity, as soon as anyone has confidence in his own strength, he will inflict whatever he wishes on those weaker than himself, and treat goodness, shame and good faith as empty words; and will have no other motive to do right than the sense of his own weakness.

The internal cohesion of states also would be perpetually insecure if religion were abolished; fear of temporal punishment would certainly not suffice to keep the citizens to their duty, nor loyalty pledged to their superior, nor the glory of being faithful to their allegiance, nor gratitude that his sovereign power protects them from the miseries of the natural state. For without religion the saying would apply, 'He who knows how to die cannot be forced.'[1] For those who

---

[1] *Cf.* Seneca, *Hercules furens*, 426.

do not fear God have nothing worse to fear than death, and anyone who had the courage to despise death could make any attempt he pleased against the government. And there might always be reasons why he would wish to do so. He might wish for instance to avoid the disadvantages he perceives himself to suffer from being ruled by someone else; or he might aim to win for himself the advantages he sees falling to the possessor of power, particularly since he may easily persuade himself that he has a right to do so, either because the present sovereign seems to be running the country badly or because he expects to govern far better himself. An opportunity for making such an attempt might easily arise: if the king fails to protect his own life with sufficient care (and who will 'guard the guardians themselves'[2] in such a state of affairs?), or if there were a major conspiracy, or if in a condition of external war he made the enemy his ally. There is the further point that citizens would be very ready to inflict injury on each other. Since judgement is given in courts of law on the basis of actions and what can be proved, crimes and misdemeanours of a profitable nature that could be committed in secret and without witnesses, would be taken as evidence of smart thinking on which one could pride oneself. And no one would practise works of mercy and friendship unless he had assurance of glory or reward. And as no one could be certain of another's good faith if there were no divine punishment, men would live in anxiety, a perpetual prey to fear and to suspicions that they would be deceived or wronged by others. Rulers as well as subjects would be disinclined to do great and glorious things. For without the bond of conscience rulers would treat all their duties, and justice itself, as available for a price, and would look to their own interest in everything and oppress their citizens. Living in constant fear of rebellion, they would realize that their only hope of security lay in making their citizens as weak as possible. The citizens for their part, fearing oppression by their rulers, would be constantly on the watch for opportunities of revolt, and would equally distrust each other and live in mutual fear. On even the smallest quarrel, husbands would suspect that their wives would use poison or some other clandestine means of death against them, and wives would suspect their husbands. A similar danger would threaten from their dependants. For since without religion there would be no conscience,

---

[2] *Cf.* Juvenal, *Satires*, 6.347.

it would not be easy to detect secret crimes of that kind, which are usually betrayed by an unquiet conscience and by tell-tale signs of anxiety. From all this it is clear how much it is in the interest of the human race to stop up every way of atheism and prevent its growth, and what madness dogs the steps of those who aver that a readiness for impiety is the way to win a reputation for political sagacity.

5
On duty to oneself

1. Self-love is implanted deep in man; it compels him to have a careful concern for himself and to get all the good he can in every way. In view of this it seems superfluous to invent an obligation of self-love. Yet from another point of view a man surely does have certain obligations to himself. For man is not born for himself alone; the end for which he has been endowed by his Creator with such excellent gifts is that he may celebrate His glory and be a fit member of human society. He is therefore bound so to conduct himself as not to permit the Creator's gifts to perish for lack of use, and to contribute what he can to human society. So, by analogy, though a person's ignorance is his own shame and loss, yet the master is right to flog the pupil who neglects to learn such skills as his capacity allows.

2. Furthermore, man consists of two parts, soul [*anima*] and body. The soul has the function of ruler, the body of servant and instrument; consequently we employ the mind [*animus*] for government and the body for service. We must care for both, but particularly for the former. Above all the mind [*animus*] must be formed to accept social life with ease; it must be steeped in a sense and a love of duty and goodness. Every man must also receive some education in accordance with his capacity and fortune, so that no one shall be a useless burden on the earth, a problem to himself and a nuisance to others. He must also choose in due time an honest way of life in accordance with his natural bent, his mental and physical abilities, the condition of his birth, his fortune, his parents' wishes, the commands of the civil rulers, opportunity or necessity.

3. Since the mind depends upon support from the body, we must

strengthen and preserve the powers of the body with appropriate food
and exercise. We should not weaken them by intemperance in food or
drink or by unseasonable and unnecessary toil or by any other means.
For the same reason we must avoid gluttony, drunkenness, excessive
sex, and so on. Further, since powerful and disordered emotions not
only drive a man to disturb society, but also do harm to him as an
individual, an effort must be made to restrain the emotions so far as
possible. And since many dangers can be repelled if faced with spirit,
one must reject unmanliness and strengthen the mind against the fear
of danger.

4. No one gave himself life; it must be regarded as a gift of God.
Hence it is clear that man certainly does not have power over his own
life to the extent that he may terminate it at his pleasure. He is
absolutely bound to wait until He who assigned him this post commands him to leave.

Yet it may be quite correct for a man to choose what will probably
shorten his life in order to make his talents more widely available to
others. For he can and should exert himself to serve the needs of
others; and a certain kind or a certain intensity of labour may so wear
out his strength as to hasten the onset of old age and death earlier
than if he had lived a gentler life.

Again, since a citizen must often risk his own life to save the lives of
many others he may be ordered by his legitimate ruler under threat of
the severest penalties not to avoid danger by flight. He may also take
such a risk of his own accord provided that there are not stronger
arguments against it and there is reason to expect that his action will
result in safety for others and that they deserve to be saved at so high a
price. For it would be stupid to add one's own death to that of another
for no good reason, or for an outstanding individual to die for a man
of no value. In general, however, there seems to be no precept of
nature that one should prefer another's life to one's own, but other
things being equal, each may put himself first.

Nevertheless, whoever terminates or throws away his life of his own
accord must be regarded without fail as violating natural law, whether
he is driven by the common troubles of human life, or by resentment
at sufferings which would not have made them objects of scorn to
human society, or by fear of pains (where others might have profited
from his example if he had borne them with courage), or in an empty
display of faith or fortitude.

5. But though self-preservation is commended to man by the tenderest instinct and by reason, it often seems to conflict with the precept of sociality. This happens, for example, when our safety is endangered by another man so that we cannot avoid death or serious injury without injuring him in warding him off. We must therefore discuss the use of moderation in defending ourselves against others.

Self-defence, then, occurs either without injury to the party threatening us, when we make sure that an attack on us would be risky or dangerous to him, or with injury or death. There is no doubt that the former is legitimate and free of all wrong.

6. But a question may be raised about the latter, because the loss to the human race is equal whether the assailant dies or I do; and because there will in any case be loss of a fellow man with whom I am obliged to practise social life; and because violent self-defence seems to create more turmoil than if I either take flight or patiently offer my body to the attacker.

But these points do not succeed in rendering this kind of defence illegitimate. If I am to deal in a peaceful and friendly manner with someone, he must for his part show himself fit to receive such duties from me. Now the law of sociality intends men's safety; it must therefore be so interpreted as to cause no harm to the safety of individuals. Hence when another intends my death, there is no law that bids me sacrifice my own safety, so that his malice may be able to rage unchecked. If anyone is hurt or killed on such an occasion he can only blame his own wickedness which placed that necessity on me. For otherwise, all the good things which nature or industry have gained for us would be given to no purpose, if we could not resist with force anyone who unjustly attacked us; and good men would be exposed as ready spoil to the wicked, if they really ought never to meet them with force. Therefore a complete ban on self-defence by force would be the death of the human race.

7. One should not, however, always take extreme measures when injury is threatened. First try more cautious remedies: for example, to block the attacker's approach, or to shut oneself up in a protected place, or to warn the attacker to desist from his fury. It is the mark of a prudent man also to show patience at a slight injury if it is conveniently possible, and to give in a little on his own right rather than expose himself to greater danger by an ill-timed show of force, especially when the object sought is easily restored or made good.

However, when my safety cannot be achieved by this or similar means, I may proceed even to extremes to achieve it.

8. To make a clear judgement as to whether a man is within the bounds of innocent self-defence, one must first know whether he is in natural liberty not subject to any one at all, or whether he is subject to civil government.

In a state of natural liberty when a man sets out to inflict an injury on another, is untouched by repentance and refuses to give up his wicked attempt and to resume peaceful relations with me, I may even go so far as to kill him in warding off his attack. I may do this not only if he seeks my life, but also if he attempts to wound or merely hurt me, or even to steal my property without harming me physically. For I have no guarantee that he will not pass from these to greater injuries; and he who professes himself an enemy is no longer protected by any right which would prevent me from repelling him by any means whatsoever. And in fact human life would be unsociable, if one could not employ extreme measures against anyone who persisted in a series of small injuries. For these would have the effect that moderate men would always be the prey of the worst.

In this state, moreover, I may not only repel the immediate danger, but after doing so may pursue the attacker until I have a guarantee from him for the future. This is the rule of the guarantee: if anyone who has attempted an injury repents of his own accord, seeks pardon, and offers reparation for loss, I am obliged to accept his word and resume friendly relations. For it is a firm sign of a change of heart to repent of one's own accord and seek pardon. But if he does not show a change of heart until his means of resistance have run out, it seems hardly safe to trust his bare promise. One must remove from such a man the means of doing harm or put some restraint on him, to prevent him becoming formidable again in future.

9. But those who are subject to civil government are only justified in using violence in self-defence when time and place do not allow appeal to the assistance of the magistrate to repel an injury by which life or some irreplaceable good, as valuable as life itself, is thrown into immediate danger. But this is confined to repelling the danger; vengeance and a guarantee against attack in the future must be left to the judgement of the magistrate.

10. I may engage in defence against an attempt on my life, whether it is motivated by malice or made in error – for example, if a man

attacked me in a fit of madness or because he took me for someone else with whom he was on terms of enmity. For it is enough that the other has no right to attack or to kill me, and that there is no obligation on my part to submit to death for no reason.

11. With regard to the time within which defence may rightly be made, this is what we must hold. Where both parties are in natural liberty, though they may and should presume that others will observe the duties of natural law towards them, yet because of the wickedness of the human heart, they should never feel so secure that they do not surround themselves in good time with innocent defences, for example by erecting obstacles to the approach of those who have hostile designs; by collecting arms and men; by forming alliances; by keeping a good watch on others' movements, and so on. But this suspicion which arises from men's common wickedness does not justify me, under cover of self-defence, in taking the initiative in conquering another by force, not even if I see his power growing inordinately, especially when he has increased it by innocent industry or by the kindness of fate without oppressing others.

If someone displays the capacity and the will to do harm not against me but against a third party, I may not immediately take the initiative of attacking him in my own name, unless it is a case of being bound by treaty to give help to a party unjustly attacked by a stronger power. It is in my interest to do this all the more promptly if it is probable that after conquering the other, he will turn on me and use his first victory as a means to the next one.

When it is quite clear that he is engaged in planning violence against me, even though he has not fully revealed his design, I shall be justified in immediately initiating self-defence by force, and in seizing the initiative against him while he is still making preparations, if there is really no hope that a friendly warning would induce him to drop his hostile design, or if such a warning would damage my own position. Hence the aggressor will be taken to be the party which first conceived the intention to harm the other and prepared himself to achieve it; but the goodwill of being a defender will go to him who by moving quickly got the better of an opponent who was rather slow to get ready. For to have the name of defender it is not necessary to suffer the first blow or merely to elude and repel the blows aimed at one.

12. In states, by contrast, self-defence is not given such a broad

scope. For it is never permitted in a state to get in the first blow against a fellow citizen, even though I am aware that he is preparing to use force against me or is broadcasting outrageous threats. Rather he will have to be brought before our common ruler, and guarantee be sought from him. Only when a man is already being attacked by another and is reduced to such straits that he has no chance of imploring the aid of the magistrate or of his fellow citizens, may he meet the violence of his assailant with extreme measures, and not with the intention of getting revenge for the injury by killing, but because his life cannot be saved from imminent danger without such a killing.

This is how one may determine the moment when one may first kill another in one's own defence with impunity: when the attacker, making obvious his intention to seek my life and equipped with strength and weapons to injure, is already within range to do harm and inflict actual injury, taking into account the distance I need, if I prefer to attack first rather than be attacked. But a modest excess would not be a matter of concern in a human court because of the mental turmoil that such great danger causes.

The period of innocent self-defence lasts until the assailant has been driven off, or has withdrawn freely, either because he was touched by repentance in the moment of action or because he has not succeeded in his attempt, so that he cannot do any more harm for the present and I have an opportunity to get to a safe place. For vengeance for injury and guarantee for the future belong to the office and authority of the civil government.

13. Despite the dictum that one is not justified in resorting to killing when the danger can be averted in a milder manner, it is not usual to be scrupulous about details because of the mental turmoil caused by imminent danger. For a person panicking in such danger cannot carefully look around for all the ways of escape as one might who considers the situation with a calm mind. Hence, although it is reckless to leave a safe place of one's own accord to meet a challenger, yet, if my attacker catches me in an open spot, I am not positively obliged to flee, unless there happens to be a refuge in the neighbourhood to which I can withdraw without danger, and even then I am not always obliged to retreat. For even in that case I would have to expose an unprotected back, and in both cases there would be the risk of a fall, and when one has once lost his footing, it is not easy to recover it.

Further, one is not barred from the plea of self-defence because he has chosen to appear in public to go about his business, when he would have been safe from danger if he had remained at home. But he does not enjoy the same plea if he presents himself to take part in a duel to which he has been challenged and is so hard-pressed that he can only avoid being killed by running his opponent through. For since the laws forbid one to put oneself in that danger, it is not accepted as an excuse for killing.

14. In defence of his limbs a man is allowed the same as in defence of his life; consequently he would be held innocent who killed a violent assailant, whose intention perhaps was merely to mutilate a limb or to inflict a severe wound. For it is natural for us to flinch right away from mutilation and serious wounds; and mutilation, particularly of one of the major limbs, is sometimes held to be not much less serious than the loss of life itself. In fact, it is never clear in advance whether death may not follow a mutilation or wound; such forbearance goes beyond men's normal fortitude, and the laws do not generally bind one to show such forbearance, especially for the benefit of an evil man.

15. What one may do to protect life, one is also usually judged to be entitled to do in defence of female virtue. No greater insult can be offered to a good woman than to attempt to take from her against her will that in whose integrity chiefly lies the reputation of her sex, and to put her in the position of being forced to raise a child of her own blood for an enemy.

16. Among those who live in natural liberty the defence of property extends to the killing of the attacker, provided the property is of some value. For we certainly cannot preserve our lives without property; and a wrongful attack on property reveals as hostile an intention as an attack on our lives.

On the other hand, this is not normally allowed in states, where stolen goods can be recovered with the help of the magistrate, except in the case where one who has come to steal our goods cannot be brought to justice. In view of this, it is lawful to kill burglars by night and robbers.

17. So much for self-defence on the part of those who are wrongfully attacked without provocation. By contrast, one who has done previous harm to another is barred from defending himself and doing further harm to the other in his defence, until certain conditions have been fulfilled. He must be moved to repent and must have offered repar-

ation for the damage he has done and a guarantee that he will do no harm in future; and the injured party must have refused his offer in the savagery of his heart and insist on obtaining vengeance with his own hand.

18. Finally, self-preservation is valued so highly that it is held to exempt a man in many cases from the obligation of the common laws, if that is the only way it can be secured. For this reason, 'necessity', it is said, 'knows no laws'.

Since man values his own preservation so highly, one does not readily presume that any obligation has been imposed on him which should take precedence over his own safety. Admittedly, not only God but also the civil government may impose on us, where the gravity of the matter requires it, so strict an obligation, that we must face death rather than be at all deficient in our duty. But legal obligations are not presumed to be always so strict. For those who made the laws and those who have introduced customs have certainly wished to promote men's security or convenience in this way; hence they are usually thought to have had the condition of human nature before their eyes, and how man cannot but avoid and avert what tends to his own destruction. Consequently laws, particularly positive laws, and all human customs are generally regarded as making an exception of the case of necessity, or as not imposing an obligation whose fulfilment would entail distress destructive of human nature or beyond the capacity of normal human nature to endure, unless this is included in the law, either expressly or by the nature of the activity. Hence necessity does not cause the law to be directly broken, nor cause wrong to be permitted; rather it is presumed, from the benevolent intention of the legislator and taking account of human nature, that the case of necessity is not included in the general scope of the law. This will be made plain by one or two examples.

19. One has normally no right over one's own limbs, to mutilate or destroy them at will; one may, however, amputate a limb infected with an incurable disease to save the rest of the body, to prevent infection of parts that are still healthy or to stop the use of the other limbs from being impeded by a useless appendage.

20. If in a shipwreck more men have leapt into a lifeboat than it can carry and the lifeboat does not belong to one of them by any particular right, it seems one should draw lots as to who should be thrown

overboard, and anyone who refuses to take his chance in the lottery may be tossed out in any case without reference to the draw, on the ground that he intends the death of all of them.

21. If two men are in immediate danger of both perishing, one is allowed to do anything to hasten the death of the other (since the other would perish anyway) in order to save himself. For example, suppose I as a swimmer had fallen into deep water with someone who could not swim, and he clung about me and held me, but I had not the strength to get him out of the water as well as myself, I may use force to disengage him from me, to prevent my being drowned along with him, even though I might have held him up somehow for a little while.

Similarly in a shipwreck, suppose I have got hold of a plank which cannot carry two, if someone swims up with the intention of getting on to the plank with me, thus destroying both of us together, I may use any amount of force to keep him away from the plank.

Similarly when an enemy who is threatening death is pressing upon two persons who are fleeing, the one may leave the other in danger of his life, either by closing a gate behind himself or by breaking down a bridge, if both cannot be saved together.

22. Necessity justifies the indirect exposure of another person to risk of death or severe injury, provided that it was not our intention to harm him, but only to do for our own safety an act which might cause him harm; provided also that we would have preferred to handle our emergency in some other way, and that we minimize the actual injury as much as possible. For example, suppose I am being pursued by a stronger man than myself who intends my death, and by chance someone meets me in a narrow way by which I must flee; if he does not give way after a warning, or if there is no time or the spot is too narrow for him to give way, I may knock him flat and pursue my flight across his prostrate body, though in all probability he is likely to be badly hurt by the blow. (There would be an exception to this if I were bound to him by a particular obligation, so that I ought to incur danger on his behalf of my own accord.) But if the man who blocks my flight cannot get out of the way despite a warning, for example, if he is an infant or a cripple, there will at least be some excuse for the pursued, if he attempts to jump over him to avoid getting involved in a delay and so exposing his body to his enemy. On the other hand, if someone wilfully and unkindly obstructs me and refuses to clear the path of my flight, he may be hit and flattened directly. And those who

receive injury by such accidents should bear them as fated misfortunes.

23. Anyone who through no fault of his own is in extreme want of food or clothes to protect him against the cold and has not succeeded by begging, buying or offering his services in persuading those who have wealth and abundance to let him have them of their own accord, may take them by force or stealth without committing the crime of theft or robbery, especially if he has the intention of repaying their value when he has the opportunity. For a rich man ought to help someone in that kind of necessity as a duty of humanity. Though what is due on the basis of humanity may absolutely not be taken by force in normal circumstances, still extreme necessity has the effect of providing a right to such things no less than to things which are due on the basis of perfect obligation. However, the necessary conditions are: that the man in want first try all other ways to satisfy his needs with the consent of the owner; that the owner is not now caught in and not soon likely to fall into equally dire straits; and that restitution be made, especially when the other's fortunes do not allow him to make a free gift of his aid.

24. Finally, an emergency affecting our own property seems to give one leave to destroy another person's property. The conditions are: that the danger to our property is not our fault; that it cannot be removed in a more convenient way; that the other man's property which we are destroying is not more valuable than ours which we are saving; that we pay the value of that property, if it would not otherwise have perished, or make up some part of the loss if his property would otherwise have perished or its loss saves ours. This is the principle of equity which maritime laws follow. Thus if a fire has broken out and is threatening my house, I may pull down my neighbour's house; the condition is that those whose houses are saved in this way make good the neighbour's loss pro rata.

6

On the duty of every man to every man, and first of not harming others

1. We come now to the duties which a man must perform towards other men. Some result from the common obligation by which the Creator has willed that all men be bound as men; others derive from a particular custom which has been introduced or accepted, or from a particular adventitious state. The former are to be shown by every man to every man, the latter only towards certain men on the basis of a particular condition or state. Hence you may call the former absolute, the latter hypothetical.

2. First among the absolute duties is the duty not to harm others. This is at once the most far-reaching of all duties, extending as it does to all men as men, and the easiest, since it consists of mere omission of action, except insofar as passions in conflict with reason must sometimes be restrained. It is also the most essential duty, since without it human social life would be utterly impossible. For I can live at peace with a man who does me no positive service, and with a man who does not exchange even the commonest duties with me, provided he does me no harm. In fact, this is all we desire from mankind at large; it is only within a fairly small circle that we impart good things to each other. By contrast, there is no way that I can live at peace with one who does me harm. For nature has implanted in each man such a tender love of himself and of what is his, that he cannot but repel by every means one who offers to do harm to either.

3. This duty affords protection not only to what we have from nature, as life, body, limbs, chastity, liberty, but also to what we have acquired on the basis of some institution and human convention. Hence this precept forbids that anything which is ours by legitimate title be taken,

spoiled, damaged or removed from our use in whole or in part. By this precept all crimes are understood to be forbidden by which harm is inflicted on another, as, killing, wounding, beating, robbery, theft, fraud and other forms of violence, whether inflicted directly or indirectly, in person or through an agent.

4. From this it follows that harm inflicted on one man by another, or loss of any kind caused in any way, must be made good so far as possible by the person who may rightly be held responsible. Otherwise the precept that one should not be harmed will be empty if when a man has in fact been harmed, he has to absorb the loss without recompense while the culprit enjoys the fruit of his crime in security and without making restitution. Again, without the necessity of making restitution, men in their wickedness will not refrain from harming each other; and the one who has suffered loss will not readily bring himself to make peace with the other as long as he has not obtained compensation.

5. Though the concept of loss properly belongs to harm to property, we take it here in a broad sense as signifying all harm, spoiling, curtailment or removal of what is ours, or usurpation of what we ought by perfect right to have had, whether it was a gift of nature or assigned to us by a supervening human act or law, or finally the omission and refusal of some payment that another party was obliged to make to us on a basis of perfect right. But if what is usurped was due only by an imperfect obligation, it is not considered to be a loss requiring compensation. For it would be inappropriate if I considered it a loss and demanded compensation for not having received what I could expect from another only as a voluntary favour, and which I could not treat as my property before I had actually received it.

6. The term loss applies not only to harm, destruction or theft of our property, but also to the fruits that arise from the property, whether they have already been collected, or are only anticipated (provided that the owner was intending to collect them). In this case the expenses which would have been necessary for collecting the fruits are deducted. The value of the expected fruits is higher or lower as they are nearer or farther from the end of their probable growth.

Finally, any loss which arises subsequently as by natural necessity from an act of harming is treated as part of a single loss.

7. One can inflict loss on another, not only directly oneself, but also by means of others.

If one has inflicted loss directly, another man can be held partly responsible for it, because he has contributed to the fact either by positive action, or by failing to do what he should have done.

Sometimes where more than one person has conspired in the same fact, one is held to be the principal cause, the other an accessory; sometimes all are on an equal footing.

In this case, one must note that those persons are held liable to make reparation for the loss who really were a cause of the loss and contributed significantly to the total loss or part of it. But a man will not be held liable to make reparation for a loss (even if he has committed some crime in the course of that act), where he did not play any real part in the action which gave rise to the loss, nor caused it to be done, nor profited from it subsequently. Examples are those who rejoice in the misfortunes of others, those who approve or excuse the damage after it is done, those who express a wish for it beforehand, and those who during its commission endorse and applaud it.

8. When several men have conspired in a single act resulting in a loss, the primary responsibility lies with the party who set the others on to it either by command or by some other means involving compulsion. The actual perpetrator of the crime who could not refuse his services will have the role only of an instrument.

Anyone who has participated without compulsion in the commission of a crime, or anyone who has committed a crime himself, will be held primarily responsible; secondarily, others who contributed anything to it.

If several men in conspiracy have committed a crime, each one is responsible for all of them, and all for each one; so that if all are caught, each individual must contribute a proportionate part to make good the loss. If only one is caught and the rest escape, he will be obliged to pay for all of them. When some of those caught are unable to pay, those among them with wealth will be liable for the whole sum. But if several participate in the same crime without conspiracy, and it can be clearly discovered how much each contributed to the loss, each will be obliged to make compensation only for what resulted from his own action. And if one pays the whole sum, the rest will no longer be liable for restitution of loss.

9. The obligation to make restitution for loss arises not only from harm done with intentional malice but also from harm done by negligence or by easily avoidable fault, without direct intention. For it is

not the least important element in sociality to act with such caution that our behaviour is not dangerous or intolerable. There is also often a particular obligation compelling one to employ a strict standard of care, and even the lightest fault may be enough to require restitution. This is not the case, however, if the nature of the business does not admit of a very strict standard of care; or if the fault is rather in the one who suffers than in the one who inflicts loss; or if great confusion or the circumstances of the case do not allow a high degree of carefulness, for example, if a soldier brandishing his weapons in the heat of battle wounds the comrade next to him.

10. A man who does harm by accident and without fault on his part is not obliged to make reparation. Since nothing has been done for which he could be held responsible, there is no reason why he rather than the sufferer should pay for the mischance.

11. It is also agreeable to natural equity that if loss is occasioned to another by my slave, without fault on my part, I either make it good or surrender the slave to the injured party. For a slave is naturally in any case liable to make good any loss he causes. But he has no goods of his own, from which reparation could be made, and secondly his body belongs to his owner. The fair thing, therefore, is for the owner either to make good the loss or to surrender the slave. Otherwise a slave would have licence to harm anybody as he pleased, if restitution could not be obtained either from himself because he has nothing (not even himself), nor from his owner. No matter how much his owner may beat or imprison him in punishment for his mischief, that gives no satisfaction to the victim.

12. It seems reasonable that the same thing hold good of animals in my possession. When they have caused loss to another, without fault on my part, if they were acting spontaneously and contrary to the nature of the species, the owner should make good the loss or surrender the animal. For if I had been harmed by an animal in its natural liberty, I could always do something to make up my loss by capturing or killing it; it does not seem that this right can have been taken away simply because the animal is now owned by someone. And since the owner gets profit from the animal, and the restitution of loss takes precedence over the acquisition of profit, there is clearly a legitimate claim against the owner of an animal to make good the loss, or if it is not worth that much to him, to surrender it for the offence.

13. To sum up, one who has caused loss to another without inten-

tional malice is bound to offer reparation and to give evidence that there was no malice in his action, so that the victim will not regard him as an enemy and attempt retaliation. However, one who has harmed another maliciously is not only obliged to offer reparation of his own accord, but also to evince repentance for his actions and seek pardon. In turn, if the victim obtains reparation, he is obliged to grant pardon to one who seeks it in penitence and to return to good terms with him. Anyone who refuses to be content with reparation and repentance, and insists in any case on seeking vengeance on his own account, is merely gratifying the bitterness of his own heart and destroying peace among men for no good reason. On this ground vengeance too is condemned by natural law, since its only aim is to give trouble to those who have done us harm, and to console our hearts with their pain. It is the more appropriate that men forgive each other's offences, the more frequently they violate the laws of the supreme Deity and have themselves daily need of pardon.

7
On recognizing men's natural equality

1. Man is an animal which is not only intensely interested in its own preservation but also possesses a native and delicate sense of its own value. To detract from that causes no less alarm than harm to body or goods. In the very name of man a certain dignity is felt to lie, so that the ultimate and most effective rebuttal of insolence and insults from others is 'Look, I am not a dog, but a man as well as yourself.' Human nature therefore belongs equally to all and no one would or could gladly associate with anyone who does not value him as a man as well as himself and a partner in the same nature. Hence, the second of the duties of every man to every man is held to be: that each man value and treat the other as naturally his equal, or as equally a man.

2. This equality among men consists not only in the fact that the physical strength of adult men is nearly equal to the extent that even a relatively weak man can kill a stronger man by taking him by surprise or by use of cunning and skill in arms, but also in that one must practise the precepts of natural law towards another and one expects the same in return, even though he may be better provided by nature with various gifts of mind and body; his superiority does not give him licence to inflict injuries on others. On the other hand neither the scanty provision of nature nor the niggardliness of fortune in themselves condemn one to have less access to the enjoyment of the common law than others. But what one may require or expect from others, the same, other things being equal, they should have from him; and any law [jus] that a man has made for others, it is particularly fitting that he follow himself. For the obligation to cultivate social life with others lies on all men equally; and it is not allowed to one more

than any other to violate natural laws where another person is concerned. There is no lack of popular sayings illustrating this equality: for example we are all descended from the same stock; we are all born, nourished and die in the same manner; God has given no man a guarantee of lasting and unshakeable good fortune. Likewise the teaching of Christianity is that God's favour is won not by noble birth or power or wealth, but by sincere piety, which may exist as well in the low-born as in the highly-placed.

3. It follows from this equality that he who wants to use the services of others to his own advantage must be ready to make himself useful to them in return. For anyone who requires others to serve him, but expects to be free of demands from them, surely regards others as not equal to himself.

Hence those who readily allow all men what they allow themselves are the best fitted for society. By contrast, they are altogether unsocial who suppose themselves superior to others, demand total licence for themselves alone and claim honour above others and a special share of the world's goods, when they have no special right above others. Hence this too is among the common duties of natural law, that no one require for himself more than he allows others, unless he has acquired some special right to do so, but allow others to enjoy their own right equally with him.

4. The same equality indicates how one should proceed when a right has to be distributed among others, namely to treat them as equals and to favour neither party over the other beyond the merits of the case. For otherwise the party slighted feels himself wronged and insulted, and diminished in the dignity given him by nature.

Hence it follows that common property is to be distributed among equals in equal portions. When the thing does not admit of division, those whose right to it is equal should use it in common as much as each wants, if there is enough of it. If there is not enough, they should use it in a prescribed manner, and in proportion to the number of users. One can devise no other way of observing equality. But if the object cannot be divided or held in common, they should use it in turn, or if even this will not work, or if an equivalent cannot be given to the rest of them, the thing will have to be assigned to one of them by lot. For in such cases, no more satisfactory solution can be found than chance; for it obviates the sense of contempt and leaves the dignity of the loser intact.

5. One sins against this duty through pride. In pride one prefers oneself to others for no reason at all or no good reason, and looks down on them as unequal to oneself. We say 'for no reason'. For when a person has duly won the right to put himself above others, he is justified in exercising and protecting his right, though without empty scorn or contempt of others. So, from the opposite angle, one is justified in giving another the precedence and honour which are his due. In general, a certain honest humility is the constant companion of true good breeding. It consists in reflection on the weakness of our own nature, and on the mistakes we could have made or will make in future, which are no fewer or smaller than others may make. The result is that we do not put ourselves above anyone, considering that others may use their free will as well as we and equally have this power. The right use of his free will is the one thing a man may call his own; it is the only thing on which he may value or despise himself. To set a great value on oneself without cause is truly a ridiculous fault, both because it is stupid in itself to have a high idea of oneself for nothing, and because it takes other people for fools as if they would put a high value on you for no reason.

6. It is a still greater wrong to give signs of contempt for others by deeds, words, looks, laughter or slighting gesture. This sin is to be regarded as worse, in that it vigorously excites the hearts of others to violent anger and desire for revenge. In fact there are many men who would prefer to expose their lives to instant danger, to say nothing of disturbing the public peace, rather than let an insult go unavenged. The reason is that fame and reputation are sullied by insult; and to keep their reputation intact and unsullied is very dear to men's hearts.

8

On the common duties of humanity

1. The third of the duties owed by every man to every man, to be performed for the sake of common sociality, is: everyone should be useful to others, so far as he conveniently can. For nature has established a kind of kinship among men. It is not enough not to have harmed, or not to have slighted, others. We must also give, or at least share, such things as will encourage mutual goodwill.

We are useful to others, either in an indefinite way or in a definite way; and it either costs us something, or it costs us nothing.

2. Someone is being useful to others in an indefinite way when he develops his mind and body to be a source of actions useful to others, or if he makes discoveries by the acuteness of his intellect for the betterment of human life. Hence they are thought to sin against this duty who learn no honest skill but passing their lives in silence, regard their mind as no more than salt to preserve them from decay,[1] mere numbers 'born to consume the fruits of the earth'.[2] So do they who are content with their ancestral wealth, and believe they are justified in devoting themselves to idleness, because the industry of others has already assured their livelihood. So too do they 'who hoard the wealth they have won not setting aside a portion for their kin'.[3] Likewise those who, like pigs, give no one pleasure except by dying, and others of that sort, useless burdens on the earth.

3. To those who set themselves to do good to the human race, others owe duty not to be grudging nor to put obstacles in the way of their splendid endeavours. Then, even if they have no other way of repay-

---

[1] *Cf.* Cicero, *De natura deorum*, 2.160.   [2] Horace, *Epistles*, 1.2.27.
[3] Vergil, *Aenid*, 6.610f.

ing them, they will at least be extolling their memory and advancing their fame, which is the chief reward of toil.

4. It is thought to be a particularly odious act of ill will and inhumanity not to make freely available to others those good things which we can offer them without loss, labour or trouble to ourselves. Such things are normally recognized as beneficial and harmless; that is, things that help the recipient without burdening the giver. Thus I should not refuse freely running water, I should let anyone take a light from my fire, give honest advice to one who is deliberating and be kind enough to show the way to one who is lost. Similarly, if one no longer wants to keep something, because he has too much or because it is too much trouble to maintain it, why not choose to leave it intact to be useful to others (provided they are not enemies), rather than let it be spoiled? Again, it is not right to destroy food when we have had enough, or to stop up or conceal a spring of water when we have drunk our fill, or to destroy navigation guides or road signs after we have made use of them. In this category too are small gifts given to the needy by the wealthy, and kindness shown to travellers for good reason, particularly if they are involved in an accident, and things of this kind.

5. It is a higher degree of humanity to give something to another freely from extraordinary benevolence, if it involves expense or labour to give it and it relieves his needs or is exceptionally useful to him. Such services are called benefits in a paradigmatic sense and are the fittest material for winning a reputation if duly governed by magnanimity and good sense.

The amount of these benefits and their distribution depend on the condition of the giver and of the recipient. The caution to be observed here is that our generosity should not actually do harm to those whom we think we are helping and to others; that our kindness should not exceed our capacity; that we should take into account each man's dignity and should give above all to those who are deserving; and that we should give where our help is needed and with due regard for the degree of personal relationship. One must also take note of what each most needs and what he could or could not get with or without our help. And the way in which the gifts are given adds much to the benefits, if we give with a cheerful demeanour, promptly and with expressions of goodwill.

6. In return a man who has received a benefit should be grateful; this

is how he shows that he appreciated it, and for this reason he has goodwill for the giver and seeks an opportunity to make an equal or larger repayment, as he can. For it is not necessary for us to return the exact value that was given; often willingness and effort help to fulfil the obligation. It is assumed that there is nothing which would negate the claim to have done someone a benefit. For I owe nothing to someone for pulling me out of the water if he threw me in in the first place.

7. But the more apt a benefit is to attach a man's heart to the giver, the keener is the obligation for the recipient to return the favour. At least we should not allow one who had enough confidence in us to go ahead and confer a benefit on us to be worse off for it, nor should we accept a benefit unless we plan to ensure that the giver will not have cause to regret his gift. For if there was a special reason why we particularly did not wish to be obligated, we should have tactfully refused the offer. And certainly, apart from the necessity of returning a favour, it would be irrational for anyone rashly to throw away his property and to confer a benefit which he sees will bring no return. In this way all goodwill and confidence among men would be abolished, and with them all benevolence, and there would be no freely given assistance and no initiative to earn gratitude.

8. Although an ungrateful heart is not an offence in itself, still a name for ingratitude is regarded as baser, more odious and more detestable than a name for injustice. For it is felt to show a thoroughly low and mean spirit to reveal oneself as unworthy of the judgement which another man had made of one's sense of honour; and to let it be seen that one cannot be moved to conceive a sense of humanity by benefits which soften even the beasts.

However, no action is given in the law courts for mere ingratitude, or when one simply forgets a benefit and neglects to return it, given the opportunity to do so. For the best feature of a benefit would be lost if an action were given, for example, for recovery of a sum of money; it would immediately turn into a loan. And though it is a most honourable thing to return a favour, it ceases to be so markedly honourable if it is compulsory. Finally all the law courts together would scarcely be adequate to handle this one law because of the very great difficulty of weighing the circumstances which heighten or lessen the benefit. The very reason why I conferred the benefit (that is, why I did not stipulate for repayment of what I had given) was that the other person might have the opportunity of showing that he returned the favour from a love of goodness, not from fear of punishment or compulsion; and that I for my part might be seen to have gone to this expense not in hope of gain but as an act of humanity, since I did not want to take security for repayment. And anyone who not only fails to repay a benefit but actually returns his benefactor evil for good should be punished for this action; the severity of his punishment should accord with the extent of the ingratitude he has shown.

9
On the duty of parties to agreements in general

1. Agreements [*pacta*] form a kind of bridge between the absolute and the hypothetical duties. For all duties, apart from those already discussed, seem to presuppose agreements, whether express or tacit. This then is the place to discuss the nature of agreements and what should be observed by those entering into them.

2. It is quite clear that men had to enter into agreements with each other. For although duties of humanity pervade our lives, there is no way that one could derive from that source alone every benefit that men might legitimately expect to receive from each other to their mutual advantage. In the first place, not everyone has such goodness of heart that from sheer humanity he would be willing to give others whatever would do them good without looking for an equal return. Again, benefits we might derive from others are often such that we cannot without a feeling of shame require them to be simply given to us. Often too it is not appropriate to our person or position to be beholden to another for such a kindness, so that just as the other is unable to give, so we are unwilling to accept, unless he takes something equal from us in return. Finally, it happens from time to time that others are simply not aware how they may serve our ends.

It was therefore necessary for men to make agreements with each other so that the duties which they perform for each other (and this is the advantage of sociality) might be performed more frequently and in accordance with what one might call fixed rules. This is particularly true of the mutual provision of the sort of things which a man could not surely count on getting from others on the basis of the law of humanity alone. Hence a prior determination had to be made as to what one man should do for another and what he should expect in return and might claim in his own right. This is done by means of promises and agreements.

3. The general duty imposed by natural law in this matter is that every man must keep his faith given, or fulfil his promises and agreements. For without this, we would lose most of the possible advantage of mutual exchange of services and things. And if there were no necessity to keep promises, one would not be free to form one's plans with confidence in the aid of other men. Moreover, justified causes of conflict and war are likely to be generated from the deception of trust. For when I make a performance on an agreement, if the other party breaks faith, my property or effort is lost to me. And even if I have yet performed nothing, it is still a nuisance that my plans and purposes are upset, since I could have arranged my affairs some other way, if he had not interfered. It also hurts my dignity to be made a fool of because I believed the other to be a good, reliable man.

4. One must also take note that what is due on the basis of the duty of humanity alone, differs from what is due on an agreement or on a perfect promise, above all in the following point. It is indeed right to make requests on the basis of humanity and honourable to grant them, but I may not compel the other party to performance by force either on my own part or on the part of a superior, if he neglects to perform of his own accord; I may only complain of his inhumanity, of his boorishness or insensibility. But I may resort to compulsion when what is due by a perfect promise or agreement is not freely forthcoming. Hence we are said to have an imperfect right [*jus imperfectum*] to the former, a perfect right [*jus perfectum*] to the latter, and similarly to be imperfectly obligated in the former case, perfectly obligated in the latter.

5. We pledge our faith either by a solitary or 'unilateral' act or by a reciprocal or 'bilateral' act. For sometimes one person alone binds himself to perform something; sometimes two or more people oblige themselves to do something. The former act is called a gratuitous promise, the latter an agreement.

6. Promises may be divided into imperfect and perfect. It is the former when we who promise do indeed intend to be obligated, but do not give a right to the other party to require performance or do not intend to be compelled by force to fulfil our promise. For example, I may couch my promise as follows: 'I have solemnly resolved to do this

or that for you, and I beg you to believe me.' For in this case I seem to be obligated rather by the law of veracity than by that of justice, and I prefer that the motive of my doing my duty seem to be my own constancy and dignity, rather than the other man's right. This is the case with the promises of powerful or influential men, by which they commit themselves not by words of honour, but in earnest, to a recommendation, an intercession, promotion or vote. Such a man by no means intends these things to be required of him as of right, but desires them to be wholly imputed to his humanity and veracity. So that the gratitude for the duty he has done may be the greater, the less compulsion there is in it.

7. It is a perfect promise, however, when I not only intend in fact to be obligated, but also confer a right upon another to demand what I promised as quite simply owed to him.

8. Our unconstrained consent is most particularly required, if our promises and agreements are to oblige us to give or do anything where we previously had no obligation, or to refrain from doing something which we could previously do of right. For since the fulfilment of any promise or agreement is associated with some burden, the most relevant reason why we may not rightly complain of it is that we freely consented to something which we could have avoided.

9. Consent is usually expressed by signs, such as spoken words, writing and nods. But it sometimes happens that it is plainly inferred without these signs from the actual nature of the transaction and other circumstances. For instance, sometimes silence taken together with certain particular circumstances has the force of a sign which expresses consent. Hence too the category of tacit agreements, that is, when our consent is not expressed by signs of the kind that are normally accepted in human communication, but is plainly inferred from the nature of the transaction and other circumstances. So too a principal agreement often has attached to it a tacit agreement which flows from the very nature of the transaction. And it is quite normal that in agreements certain tacit exceptions and necessary conditions are to be understood.

10. To give clear assent, a person needs the use of reason to the extent that he understands whether the transaction in question suits him, and whether he can perform his part, and after giving it thought, can express his consent by adequate signs.

It follows that the promises and agreements of infants, as well as of the demented and the insane (except when their insanity is punctuated by lucid intervals), are void.

The same pronouncement is to be made also on those who are drunk, if the drunkenness has got to the point that their reason is plainly overwhelmed and put to sleep. For it cannot be taken for true and deliberate consent, if a man veers towards something (however violently) under the influence of a momentary and unconsidered impulse, or gives out certain signs which would express consent in other circumstances, at a time when his mind has been unhinged as by a drug. It would also be shameless to try to extract such a promise, especially if fulfilling it would be a great burden. If anyone has taken advantage of that sort of drunkenness, and has smartly elicited a promise by waiting till the other party was easy of access, he will be liable to a charge of deception and fraud. But anyone who after shaking off his intoxication confirms what he did in drunkenness will certainly be obligated, not so much for what he did when drunk as for what he did when sober.

11. One cannot define precisely by natural law how long the infirmity of reason lasts in children (this is an impediment to contracting an obligation), since judgement matures earlier in some than in others. One must assess it on the basis of daily actions in each case. However, in most states the civil laws have laid down a uniform age in this matter. There is also a salutary tradition in some places that it is necessary to employ the authority in contracting obligations of other men of greater prudence, until the impulsive carelessness of youth can be regarded as cooled down. For people of this age, even when they understand the business on hand, are often carried away by attacks of impetuosity, they show little foresight, make promises lightly, are full of hope, keen to get a reputation for generosity, prone to the ostentatious cultivation of friendships and incapable of diffidence. And so there is usually a suspicion of fraud about anyone who battens on the easy-going manners of people of that age and seeks to get rich by young people's spending, which in the weakness of their judgement they do not know how to foresee or calculate.

12. Consent is also impeded by mistake. These are the rules to notice:

(1) When I have made a promise upon a mistaken assumption and if I would not have made the promise except for that assumption,

there will naturally be no force in the promise. For a promisor consents upon an assumption, and if the assumption is not so, the promise too is null.

(2) If I have been induced by a mistake to make an agreement or contract, and I discover it while the situation is unchanged and before any performance has been made, it would of course be fair to allow me the opportunity of changing my mind, particularly if I openly declared on entering into the agreement the cause which motivated me, and the other party suffers no loss from my change of mind or I am prepared to compensate him. But when the situation is no longer unchanged and when the mistake has only surfaced after the agreement has been fulfilled, either in full or in part, he who made the mistake will not be able to retreat from the agreement, except insofar as the other party is willing to do him a favour from simple humanity.

(3) When a mistake has occurred concerning the actual object of the agreement, the agreement is defective, not so much because of the mistake, but because it has failed to satisfy the conditions of an agreement. For in agreements the object about which the agreement is made and its qualities must be known; without this knowledge there cannot be taken to be a clear consent. Hence when the defect is discovered, the party that would have suffered injury can retreat from the contract, or compel the other party to make good the defect or even to pay for the loss caused by any wrongdoing or negligence on his part.

13. But if there has been inducement by fraud or wilful deceit to make a promise or an agreement, the situation is as follows:

(1) If a third party has employed fraud, without collusion of the party with whom we are making the agreement, the transaction will stand. We shall however be able to reclaim from the perpetrator of the fraud the benefits we would have had if we had not been deceived.

(2) If anyone has caused me by deliberate fraud to give a promise or make an agreement with him, I have no obligation to him at all on this basis.

(3) If anyone has entered into an agreement of his own accord and with clear and deliberate intent, but fraud has occurred in the actual transaction, with regard for example to the object or to its

qualities and value, the agreement will be to this extent vitiated, so that it will be at the discretion of the defrauded party either to dissolve it completely or to demand compensation for the loss.

(4) Things which are not of the essence of the transaction and which have not been expressly mentioned do not vitiate an act which has been properly drawn up in other respects, even though perhaps one of the parties silently thought of them while making the agreement or his belief was artfully sustained until the contract was concluded.

14. Fear, occurring in the context of promises and agreements, is taken in two senses: (1) as probable suspicion that we shall be deceived by the other party, either because vice of that kind is an integral part of his character or because he has given pretty clear indications of his evil intent; (2) as strong mental terror arising from a threat to inflict serious harm, if we do not give a promise or make an agreement. In the case of the former kind of fear, we must understand as follows:

(1) He who relies on the promises and agreements of a man whose regard for trust is worth nothing acts imprudently indeed, but the agreement is not rendered invalid for that reason alone.

(2) When an agreement has been made, and no new indications emerge of intended deception, withdrawal from the agreement will not be allowed on the pretext of defects known before the agreement was made. For a cause which did not prevent one from making an agreement ought not to prevent one from fulfilling it either.

(3) When clear indications emerge after an agreement has been made that the other party is planning to dupe me after I have performed my part of the bargain, I cannot be compelled to perform, until I have been given legal guarantees against that deception.

15. On the other kind of fear these are the rules to be noticed:

(1) Agreements entered into through fear inspired by a third party are valid. For in this case there is certainly no defect which would prevent the other party from acquiring a right against me on the basis of the agreement. And to have removed the fear which the third party threatens certainly deserves compensation.

(2)   Agreements entered into from fear of or respect for a legitimate power or in consideration of the authority of those to whom we are most closely bound are valid.

(3)   Agreements to which a man is compelled by force on the part of the person to whom he makes the promise or agreement are invalid. For the wrong which the other party does to me by the infliction of unjustified fear renders him incapable of claiming his right from me on the basis of that act. And since one is obliged in any case to make good a loss one has caused, the cancelling of my obligation is understood as his compensation of me for not giving the restitution which he should have given.

16. Consent must be mutual not only in agreements, but also in promises. Consequently, not only the promisor but also the recipient of the promise must consent. For when the latter does not consent, or when he has declined to accept the offered promise, the object of the promise remains with the promisor. For he who offers another something of his own does not intend to force it upon him against his will nor to render it ownerless. Consequently, if the other party does not accept, the promisor loses no part of his right to the object he has offered. But if there has been a prior request, it will be held to be still in effect unless expressly revoked; and that counts as a prior acceptance. This is on the condition that the offer corresponds to the request; if it is different, express acceptance is required, because it is often not to my advantage to accept anything but exactly what I have requested.

17. Concerning the subject-matter of promises and agreements, the requirements are that what we promise or agree to should not be beyond our power, and that we are not forbidden to do it by any law. Otherwise our promise is either foolish or immoral.

It follows that no one can oblige himself to what is impossible for him to perform. If, however, something which was thought to be possible at the time of entering into the agreement is subsequently made impossible by circumstances which do not imply fault on the part of the person entering into the agreement, the agreement will be void, provided no action has taken place upon it. When there has already been some performance by the other party, what has been advanced or its equivalent must be restored. If this cannot be done, every effort must be made to ensure that the other party suffers no loss. For in an agreement our first concern is its expressed purpose; when we cannot attain that, payment of an equivalent is sufficient: we must at least take every precaution not to suffer loss.

But he who has diminished his ability to perform by fraud or gross negligence is not only obliged to make every effort to perform, but will also be subject to a penalty as a kind of supplement.

18. It is also obvious that we cannot be obliged to perform an illegal act. For no one can validly bind himself further than he has the power. And he who forbids an action by law assuredly takes away the power of undertaking and of accepting an obligation to perform such a thing. It is in fact a contradiction to be under a binding obligation which has the force of law to do an action which by the same laws may not be done. Hence it is wrong to make a promise to do something illegal, but it is doubly wrong to fulfil it.

It also follows from this that one ought not to keep promises which will be harmful to the person to whom they are made since it is forbidden by natural law to inflict harm on another even at his own misguided wish.

If therefore an agreement has been made on an immoral matter, neither party will be bound to fulfil it. And if one party has committed an immoral act in pursuance of an agreement, the other will not be obliged to pay the price they had agreed. However, if any payment has been made for this purpose, it cannot be reclaimed, unless there also happens to be fraud or unjust enrichment.

19. Finally, and patently, promises and agreements about other people's property are void, insofar as they are subject to the direction and discretion of another's will and not our own. However, if I have made a promise to do my best to see that another person does something (where it is assumed that I am unable to command him by authority), then I am obliged to take every morally possible step to induce him to do it; and by morally possible I mean whatever the promisee can decently ask of me and that I, with respect for civility, can do.

But also I cannot make a valid promise to a third party concerning property and actions of mine over which someone has already acquired a right, except perhaps in anticipation of the expiry of his right. For he who has already transferred his right to another by prior promises or agreements has assuredly no further such right left to confer on a third party. Moreover all promises and agreements could easily be made useless, if one were allowed to enter into an agreement containing provisions which were contrary to a prior agreement and an obstacle to its fulfilment. This is the foundation of the old saying: prior in time is prior in law.

20. Beside all this, it is most important to notice that promises are couched either in pure and absolute terms or subject to a condition, meaning by the latter that the validity of the promise is conditional upon some event which depends on accident or human will.

Conditions are either possible or impossible. The former are subdivided into accidental or fortuitous, whose occurrence or non-occurrence is not in our power; discretionary or arbitrary, whose fulfilment or non-fulfilment is in the power of the recipient of the promise; and mixed, whose fulfilment depends partly on the will of him to whom it is given, partly on chance.

Impossible conditions are either physically such or morally; that is, there are certain things which nature prevents us from doing and certain things which law and morality forbid us to do. If we follow the natural simplicity of interpretation, an impossible condition negates a statement of promise. However, it may be legally possible, in a case where such a promise is appended to a serious transaction, to deem that it is not so appended, to prevent people from being cheated by means of acts that cannot result in anything.

21. Finally, we make promises and agreements not only in person, but also by means of others whom we appoint as messengers and interpreters of our will. When they have done in good faith what we mandated them to do, we have a valid obligation to those who have dealt with them as with our representatives.

22. And so we have done with the absolute duties of man as well as with those duties which form as it were a bridge to the others. All other duties presuppose either the introduction among men of some human institution which rests upon a general agreement, or some particular human state [*status*]. We specially notice three such human institutions: language-use, ownership of things and their value, and human government. We must expound each of these institutions and the duties to which they give rise.

10
On the duty of men in the use of language

1. Everyone knows how useful, how simply necessary, an instrument of human society language [*sermo*] is. Indeed, it has often been argued, on the basis of this faculty alone, that man is intended by nature to live a social life. The legitimate and profitable use of language for human society is based upon this duty prescribed by natural law: no man should deceive another by language or by other signs which have been established to express the sense of his mind [*sensa animi*].

2. A more profound grasp of the nature of language requires a knowledge of the double obligation incurred by using it whether in speech or in writing. The first is that users of any given language [*lingua*][1] must employ the same words for the same objects following the usage of that language. For since neither sounds nor particular letter-shapes naturally signify anything (for if they did, all languages or forms of writing would necessarily converge), the use of a language would become meaningless if everyone could give an object any name he wanted. To prevent this, it is necessary for a tacit agreement to be made among users of the same language to denote each thing with one particular word and not another. For without an accord on the consistent employment of sounds, it is impossible to understand from what someone says the sense of his mind. By virtue of this agreement everyone is obliged to use words in his common discourse in the sense they bear in the accepted usage of that language. It follows from this too that, although the sense of a man's mind may be at variance with

---

[1] 'Language' (in general): *sermo*; a particular language: *lingua*.

what he says, yet in the affairs of human life everyone is assumed to have meant what his words indicate, even if it deviates perhaps from the inner intention of his mind. For we can know nothing of his mind except by signs; and therefore all use of language would be rendered futile if an internal mental reservation, which each man can form as he pleases, could undermine the usual force of signs in social life.

3. The second obligation involved in the use of language is that in speaking to someone one should disclose the sense of one's mind to him in such a way that he may clearly know it. For man cannot only speak but may also be silent, and he is not bound to disclose what he has in mind to every audience on all occasions; consequently, there must be a particular obligation which imposes the necessity of speaking and of speaking in such a way that the other party may understand the sense of our mind. This obligation arises either from a specific agreement or from a common precept of natural law, or from the nature of the business which one is using speech to transact. For there often is an explicit agreement with someone that he will reveal his mind to me on some subject, for example, if I take someone as my instructor in some branch of knowledge. Often too some precept of natural law commands me to share the knowledge which I have with another, either to help him or to protect him from harm or to avoid giving cause or occasion of his being harmed. And there are times, finally, when a piece of current business in which I am involved with someone cannot be transacted without my revealing to him my opinion on it, as happens in making contracts.

4. But it is not always the case that my thoughts have to be shared with another for one or other of these reasons. And therefore it is clear that in talking with someone I am only bound to reveal what he has a right, perfect or imperfect, to hear from me. And so I may rightly conceal by silence, however pressingly questioned, what the other party has no right to get from me, and which I have no obligation to reveal.

5. Moreover, since language was invented for ourselves as well as for others, I may shape what I say to express something other than what I have in mind, when it is to my advantage and does not compromise another's right.

6. Finally, those to whom we are speaking are often so situated that it would hurt them and prevent us from achieving the good end we seek if they learned the plain truth in frank and open language. In these

cases, therefore, we may make use of a dissembling and specious language which does not directly represent to our audience our meaning and intention. For if I want to help someone, and if I have a duty to do so, I am certainly not obliged to proceed in a way which will defeat my purpose.

7. From this we may see what truth is, which good men are so strongly approved for loving: it is that our words should fairly represent the sense of our mind to a person who has the right to know it when we have a perfect or imperfect obligation to reveal it. And the purpose is that he may derive some benefit due to him from knowing the sense of our mind or that he may not suffer undue loss by being given to understand otherwise. It is also clear from this that we are not always telling a lie when we say, and say deliberately, what does not exactly correspond either with the facts or with our thoughts. Hence what we might call 'logical truth', which consists in the congruence of words with things, does not altogether coincide with 'moral truth'.

8. A lie, on the other hand, is when our language purposely makes out the sense of our mind to be other than it really is, provided that the person to whom we are talking has the right to know it and we have the obligation of ensuring that he does know it.

9. It follows from what we have said that the reproach of lying is certainly not incurred by those who use dissembling remarks and stories to children or child-like persons, so that they may more easily grasp their meaning, when they cannot take the naked truth. The same is also the case with those who employ dissembling discourse for a good end which they could not attain by plain speech: for example, to protect the innocent, placate the angry, comfort the mourning, give courage to the fearful, encourage the squeamish to take medicines, break the stubbornness of one or subvert the evil design of another, draw a veil, so to speak, of fabricated rumours over secrets of state and policies which must be kept from the knowledge of others and divert misplaced curiosity, or use the stratagem of deceiving with false stories an enemy whom we might openly injure.

10. By contrast, anyone who is bound in any case plainly to declare the sense of his mind to another does not avoid guilt if he tells only a part of the truth or deceives the other with ambiguous talk, or makes a mental reservation of some tacit restriction foreign to common usage.

I I

On the duties involved in taking an oath

1. An oath is held to lend conspicuous support to our speech and to all acts which involve speech. For it is a religious affirmation, by which we give up our claim to God's mercy or call down divine punishment if we shall not speak truth. An oath raises a presumption of truth by invoking an omniscient and omnipotent witness and avenger, because we find it hard to believe that anyone would be so impious as boldly to call down upon himself God's most heavy wrath. This is the reason why the duty of those who swear is to take the oath with reverence and to observe scrupulously what they have sworn.

2. Now the most important use and purpose of swearing is to bind men more strongly to tell the truth or to keep a promise or agreement, through fear of God who is omniscient and omnipotent. If they knowingly deceive Him, they invoke His vengeance upon themselves by swearing, when otherwise the fear that threatens them from men would not have been effective, since they would expect to be able to disregard or deflect men's devices or elude detection.

3. Since God alone is omniscient and omnipotent, it is absurd to take an oath by any object which is not believed to be divine in the sense of invoking it as witness and avenger of perjury. It often happens, however, that in taking an oath a certain object is named by which one will swear in the sense that if the swearer breaks his oath, God is to take particular vengeance on that object, since it is something very dear and valuable to the swearer.

4. In oaths, the formula by which God is described in the invocation to Him as witness and avenger must be adapted to the conviction or religious belief which the oath-taker has of God. For there is no

compulsion in an oath by a god in whom he does not believe and therefore does not fear. But no one believes he is swearing by God except in the formula or under the name contained in the precepts of his own religion, which is in his view the true one. This is also the reason why if a man swears by false gods whom he believes to be true gods, he is undoubtedly bound, and if he is false to his oath he is in fact committing perjury. For it was the general notion of deity that he had before his eyes under whatever particular form, hence in knowingly committing perjury he has, so far as in him lay, violated the reverence due to God's majesty.

5. A requisite of obligation by oath is that it be made with deliberate intention. Consequently a man will certainly not be bound by an oath if he simply enunciates it while reading it over or merely tenders its words (couched in the first person) to someone else. But one who gives the appearance of swearing in earnest will certainly be bound, whatever was going on in his mind while he was swearing. For the whole usefulness of the oath in human life would be destroyed, and so indeed would any means of binding oneself to an obligation by the use of signs, if by a tacit reservation one could prevent the act from having the effect it was designed to produce.

6. Oaths do not create a new, distinct obligation, but act as a kind of extra bond to an obligation which is valid in itself. For whenever we swear, we are assuming the existence of a duty whose non-performance would provoke divine punishment against us. This would be absurd if it were licit not to perform the underlying duty, and we were not, therefore, independently obliged to do it.

It follows that inherently vicious actions (to which one cannot be obligated) do not become obligatory by the addition of an oath. In the same way, the validity of an antecedent obligation is not abolished by a subsequent oath, nor is any right which was acquired from that obligation by another party. Hence an oath not to pay a debt is void.

Nor is there any obligation in an oath where it is established that the oath-taker had assumed some fact which was not actually the case, and would not have taken the oath, if he had not so believed, particularly if he has been led into error by fraud on the part of the recipient of the oath. Nor does one who uses unjustified fear to make me swear acquire any right from the oath to demand anything with justice from me. Further, an oath to perform an illicit act never has any force, nor an oath not to do any good act prescribed by divine or human law. Finally, an oath does not change the nature and substance of any promise or pact it accompanies. Hence an oath to do the impossible is void. A conditional promise is not converted to an absolute, or pure, promise by means of an oath. And acceptance of the promise is a requisite of sworn promises as of all others.

7. The effect of an oath is due to the invocation of God, whom cunning cannot deceive, whom no one mocks with impunity. It is therefore held not only that a more severe penalty awaits one who has broken a pledge confirmed by oath than otherwise, but also that affairs which include oaths must exclude all fraud and prevarication.

8. Oaths should not always be interpreted in a broad sense but sometimes strictly, if the subject matter seems to call for it, for example, if what is sworn is prejudicial to the other party, and the oath is supplementing a threat rather than a promise. Neither does an oath exclude tacit conditions and limitations which properly flow from the actual nature of the thing. For example, I shall incur no obligation at all if I have given someone by an oath the choice of asking for whatever he wants, and he asks for things which are wicked or absurd. For when one makes an indefinite promise to a petitioner before one knows what it is he will ask for, one assumes that he will ask for things that are good and morally possible, not things that are absurd and damaging to himself or others.

9. Note also that in oaths the sense which prevails is that of the whole utterance as understood, on his own profession, by the party which tenders the oath, i.e. the party to whom the oath is made. For the oath is given primarily for his sake, not for the sake of the swearer. Hence too it is for him to formulate the words of the oath. He should do so as clearly as possible and in such a way as to indicate himself how he understands them and in such a way that the swearer may acknowledge that he has a firm grasp of the other's meaning. The swearer should utter these words immediately and distinctly, so that he will have no opportunity for cavilling and evasion.[1]

10. The division of oaths is best drawn from the use to which they are put in social life. Some accompany promises and agreements to ensure more scrupulous observance. Some are employed to lend

---

[1] 'that so no room may be left for Cavils or Shuffling' (Tooke's translation).

weight to an assertion on an obscure matter of fact, where there is no better way to get at the truth. Such is the oath required of witnesses or those who are believed to have knowledge of another man's action. Sometimes, too, parties to a dispute resolve it by means of an oath, which may be tendered by a judge or by one of the parties.

12

On duty in acquiring ownership of things

1. It is the condition of the human body that it needs to take in its sustenance from without and to protect itself from anything that would destroy its integrity; there are also many things which relieve and enrich our lives. We may therefore safely infer that it is clearly the will of the supreme governor of the world that man may use other creatures for his own benefit, and that he may in fact in many cases kill them. This is true not only of vegetable species and such creatures as have no sense of their own destruction, but also of harmless animals which it is not wrong for men to kill and consume, even though they die in pain.

2. But in the beginning all these things are thought to have been made available by God to all men indifferently, so that they did not belong to one more than to another. The proviso was that men should make such arrangements about them as seemed to be required by the condition of the human race and by the need to preserve peace, tranquillity and good order. Hence while there were as yet few men in the world, it was understood that whatever a man had laid hold upon with the intention of making use of it for himself should be his and no one should take it from him, but the actual bodies [*corpora*] which produced those things should remain available to all without relation to anyone in particular. In the course of time, however, men multiplied and began to cultivate things which produce food and clothing. To avoid conflicts and to institute good order at this stage, they took the step of dividing the actual bodies of things amongst themselves, and each was assigned his own proper portion; a conven-

tion [*conventio*] was also made that what had been left available to all by this first division of things should henceforth be his who first claimed it for himself. In this way, property in things [*proprietas rerum*] or ownership [*dominium*] was introduced by the will of God, with consent [*consensus*] among men right from the beginning and with at least a tacit agreement [*pactum*].

3. Ownership is a right, by which what one may call the substance of a thing belongs to someone in such a way that it does not belong in its entirety to anyone else in the same manner. It follows that we may dispose as we will of things which belong to us as property and bar all others from using them, except insofar as they may acquire a particular right from us by agreement. In states, however, it is normally the case that ownership is not unrestricted in perpetuity for anyone, but is confined within fixed limits by the civil power or by arrangements and agreements of individuals with each other.

But when one thing belongs in the same manner to several persons without division it is said to be common to those several persons.

4. Things were not made property once and for all on one occasion, but successively and as the needs of mankind seemed to require. Similarly, it was not necessary for each and every thing to become property, but some things could, and others should, remain in what we might call primitive communion without detriment to the peace of the human race. It would be both inappropriate and unnecessary to set about dividing things which, however useful to men, are never consumed, so that they are open for all to use without prejudice to any one person's use of them: for instance, light, the sun's heat, air, flowing water and so on. One may also include those parts of the wide oceans, lying between the great continents, which are farthest from land, particularly as they are not only more than adequate for the most varied needs of all men, but to defend them is virtually impossible for any one people. For where a thing is of such a nature that others simply cannot be kept out, it is not only unnecessary for it to be divided or made someone's property, it would tend to provide material for pointless disputes.

5. Modes of acquiring ownership are either original or derivative. Original modes apply to the first assertion of property over a thing, while derivative modes transfer an existing ownership from one person to another. The former modes, in turn, are either merely original,

and by them one acquires ownership of the body of something, or are original only in a certain respect and by these some increment is made to a thing which is ours.

6. After men had accepted division of things by ownership, they made a convention [*conventio*] that whatever had not entered into the earliest division should go to the occupier, that is to the man who first physically laid hold of it with the intention of holding it for himself. Consequently the only original mode of acquiring ownership today is occupation [*occupatio*].

This is the mode by which unoccupied regions which no one has ever claimed are acquired. They become his who first enters them with the intention of holding them so as to introduce cultivation and establish fixed limits for the extent of the territories which he wishes to be his. Where a company of many men jointly occupy some part of the earth, the most usual thing is that some portion is assigned to individual members of the company, and the rest is taken to belong to the whole company.

Occupation is also the means of acquiring wild beasts, birds and fish that live in seas, rivers or lakes; likewise whatever the sea throws up on the shore; provided that the civil power does not forbid casual taking of such things or assign them to some definite person. For them to become ours, we must physically take them and subject them to our power.

Occupation is also the means of acquiring things whose previous ownership is clearly extinct. For example, things thrown away with the intention that they no longer be ours; or what we at first lose without wishing to, but afterwards treat as abandoned. An example of this is treasure-trove, or money whose owner is unknown; it falls to the finder, where the civil laws make no other provision.

7. Few things in ownership continue forever in the same state; most enlarge their substance by various increments. In some cases there are external increments; others bear fruits; others increase in value by being given form by human industry. All may be included in the term 'accession', and divided into two classes. One class arises from the nature of the things without human action; the other is produced in whole or in part by human action or human industry. The rule for all is: accessions and all profits belong to the owner of the thing; and whoever makes a new product out of his own material is the owner of the product.

8. But it often happens that others acquire a right (on the basis of contract or otherwise) of deriving a certain benefit from our property, or even of preventing us from using it as we might wish without restriction. These rights are normally called servitudes. They are divided into personal servitudes, where the benefit from the other person's property accrues directly to the beneficiary, and real servitudes, where the benefit from another's property is obtained by way of our own.

Included among personal servitudes are: usufruct, use, habitation and the services of slaves. Real servitudes are divided into urban and rustic praedial servitudes. Examples of urban praedial servitudes are the servitudes of bearing a beam, of lights, of not restricting light, of outlook, of accepting run-off water. Among rustic praedial servitudes are those of passage, of driving cattle, general right of way, the right of carrying water, of drawing water and of driving cattle to water, the right of grazing, etc. The general reason for these is the regulation of relations between neighbours.

9. Among the derivative modes of acquisition, there are some by which a thing is passed to another by disposition of the law, others by a prior act of the owner; and with effect either to transfer the whole of someone's goods or a certain portion thereof.

10. The whole of one's goods pass by law on the death of the previous owner in intestate succession. It is contrary to common human feeling and scarcely conducive to the peace of mankind that the goods which a man has acquired with such labour through his life be regarded as abandoned on the death of the owner and available to anyone to occupy. Reason has suggested the universally accepted custom that where a man has made no disposition of his goods, they should devolve on those whom the common feelings of humanity suggest he held most dear to him. These are normally our descendants and, next to them, our blood relations by degrees of proximity. Granted there are men who may love certain outsiders more than those of their own blood, either for benefits received or from particular affection, yet in the interests of peace one should rather follow the common inclination of mankind without regard to the personal feelings of a few individuals, and follow the mode of succession which is most obvious and not liable to complex disputes. Disputes would surely arise, if benefactors and friends could compete with those whose claim rests on the rights of blood. Anyone who

absolutely wished to prefer benefactors or friends to his relatives should have made explicit dispositions to that effect.

11. It follows that a man's nearest heirs are his children. Nature encourages parents to feed and raise their children with anxious care; every parent is supposed to want for his own the most ample provision possible, and to leave first to them whatever he does not need for himself. The term 'children' refers principally to those who are the issue of a legitimate marriage. They are favoured over natural children by reason itself, by the decency of civil life and the laws of civilized peoples. These principles hold unless the father has refused for sufficient reason to recognize someone as his son or has disinherited him for outrageous conduct. The term 'children' also includes members of the next generation. The grandparent has the duty to look after them if the parents die; likewise it is perfectly reasonable for the grandchildren to share with the uncles on both sides in their grandfather's estate. Otherwise exclusion from the grandfather's estate would be added to the tragedy of the early death of their father.

When descendants fail, it is reasonable that property should devolve on the parents of the deceased children. Brothers succeed where neither children nor parents survive. Where these too are lacking, the heir will be whoever happens to be nearest in blood to the deceased. However, we find that most states have made precise arrangements on the order of succession both to avoid legal disputes (this is a very frequent source) and to settle the matter in the public interest. The safest course for private individuals is to follow this order, unless serious reasons compel them to adopt a different disposition.

12. The testament is the means by which an estate as a whole is passed by act of the previous owner. Most peoples have adopted the custom which is itself a kind of consolation for mortality, that a man may make arrangements during his lifetime for the transfer of his property in the event of his death to the person he most loves. In the earliest times it seems to have been most usual to announce the names of one's heirs openly on the approach of death, and physically to deliver the patrimony into their hands. Later, for good reasons, most peoples adopted a different form of testament, namely that a testator might, at any time he wished, either publicly signify his last will or quietly put it into writing and seal it. He might also change the will as he wished, and the heirs, whether named in public or included in the

written will, obtained no right under it until the death of the testator. And though such last wills are rightly very popular, they must nevertheless be regulated by due regard for relatives and for the public interest. States have normally provided a standard form of testament. If a person deviates from this arrangement, there are no grounds to complain that no account was taken of his wishes.

13. The passing of property among the living by act of the previous owner occurs either gratis or by way of a contract. The first kind of transfer is called a gift. Contracts will be discussed later.

14. Sometimes too property is transferred against the will of the previous owner. In states this most often takes the form of a penalty, where sometimes the whole of an estate, sometimes a fixed part, is taken away from those convicted of wrongdoing and given either to the public or to the wronged party. Similarly in war things are taken without consent by an enemy of superior strength and become the property of the taker. The previous owner does not lose his right to use equal force to get them back until he renounces all claim to them by a subsequent treaty of peace.

15. Prescription [*usucapio*] is a particular mode of acquisition, by which one who obtained possession of something in good faith and with just title and has had peaceful and uninterrupted possession for a long time, is at length regarded as absolute owner of the thing, with the effect that he can defeat the former owner if he tries subsequently to claim it as his. One reason for introducing this right was that if the former owner had neglected to claim it for a long time he was judged to have abandoned the thing, since over a long period he must have had opportunities to reclaim it. The other reason was that it makes for peace and tranquillity if questions of possession are eventually settled beyond controversy. All the more so since it seems much more serious to be deprived after long possession of what one acquired in good faith than no longer to have what was lost long ago and is no longer even missed. It is, however, conducive to peace and tranquillity for states to establish fixed periods for completion of the process of prescription of whatever length the reason or interest of the state suggests.

13

On the duties arising from ownership in itself

1. The following are the duties which have arisen from the introduction of ownership in things:

   (1) Every man is obliged to allow everyone (except an enemy) quietly to enjoy his own property, and neither by force nor fraud to attempt to spoil, steal or misappropriate it. This is why theft, robbery and similar crimes against others' property are forbidden.

2. (2) When without crime or breach of good faith on our part another man's property comes into our hands, and we have it under our control, we are bound to do all we can to return it to the control of its legitimate owner. However, we are not bound to restore it at our own expense, and if we do spend anything on maintaining it, we may rightly recover our expense or keep the property until we are paid. The obligation of restitution begins when we become clearly aware that the property belongs to someone else. At that time we should make it known that we have the thing in question and do nothing to hinder the owner in recovering what is his [*suum*]. If, however, we have acquired something with good title, we are not obliged to cast doubt on the title ourselves, or make a kind of public announcement whether anyone wishes to claim it for himself. The duty of restitution takes precedence over particular contracts and is a ground for a counter-claim: for example, if a thief deposits stolen goods

with me and the real owner subsequently turns up, they must be restored to the owner, not the thief.

3. (3) If in good faith we have acquired something of another's and consumed it, our duty is limited to restoring to the owner the amount by which we have been enriched, so that we do not gain from another's undeserved loss.

4. The following duties are derived from the above:

    (i) A bona fide possessor is not obliged to make any restitution if the thing has perished, because he has neither the thing itself nor any gain from it.

5. (ii) A bona fide possessor is bound to make restitution not only for the thing but for any fruits still in existence. For the fruits belong by nature to the owner of the thing. The possessor may however deduct all that he has spent on the thing and its cultivation to produce the fruits.

6. (iii) A bona fide possessor is bound to make restitution for the thing and any fruits of it that have been consumed, provided that he would have consumed as much anyway, and can recover the price of the thing he must surrender from the party from whom he received it. For he has been enriched by sparing his own property while consuming another's.

7. (iv) A bona fide possessor is not bound to give compensation for fruits he has neglected to obtain. The reason is that he does not have the thing nor anything that has succeeded it.

8. (v) If a bona fide possessor receives as a gift something belonging to someone else and gives it in turn to a third party, he incurs no obligation, unless some other duty would have obliged him to make an equivalent donation in any case. For in that case he will have had the advantage of sparing expense from his own property.

9. (vi) If a bona fide possessor has in any way alienated something belonging to someone else, which he has acquired with an encumbered title, his obligation is limited to the profit he has made from it.

10. (vii) A bona fide possessor is also obliged to make restitution of something belonging to another, which he has acquired with an encumbered title, and he may not claim what he has spent on it from the owner but only from the person from

whom he received it; except to the extent that the owner could probably not have recovered possession of his property without some expense or may of his own accord have offered a reward for information.

11. Whoever finds something of another's which the owner was probably unwilling to lose, may not take it with the intention of concealing it from the owner's search. But when no owner turns up, he may rightly keep it for himself.

14
On value[1]

1. After ownership of things had been introduced, the custom of exchange soon followed. For then as now all things were not of the same nature nor had the same usefulness to human needs, and no one individual had as much for his own use as he desired. Hence it often happened that things of different nature or use needed to be passed from one person to another. To prevent either party suffering in an exchange of that kind it was necessary to assign, by agreement between men, some quantity in terms of which things could be compared and equated with each other. This was also the case with actions which one was unwilling to do for others' benefit for nothing. This quantity usually goes by the name of 'value' [*pretium*].

2. Value is divided into common value and eminent value. Common value is found in things and actions, or services, which enter into commerce because they give us use and pleasure. Eminent value is seen in money, since it is accepted as virtually containing the value of all goods and services and as providing them with a common measure.

3. The foundation of common value in itself is the suitability of the thing or service to make a direct or indirect contribution to the needs of human life and to render it fuller and more agreeable. Hence things that have no use at all are normally said to have no value.

There are, however, some things which are very useful to human life on which no definite value is understood to be set. This is because either they are and must be without ownership, or because they are incapable of being exchanged and therefore excluded from com-

---

[1] [*De Pretio*]: '*pretium*' is here normally translated as 'value', but occasionally as 'price', depending on context.

93

merce, or because in commerce they are regarded only as appendages to something else. Again, human or divine law has set certain actions apart from commerce or has forbidden them to be done for pay, and so is understood to have withdrawn them from the sphere of value. Examples are (1) no price can be put upon the upper regions of the air, the ether, the heavenly bodies and the high seas, because they are not subject to human ownership; (2) a free person has no price, because free men are not objects of trade; (3) the open light of the sun, bright clean air, a pretty countryside as a prospect for the eyes, wind, shade and so on, have no value taken by themselves alone, since man cannot enjoy them without the use of land, yet they have great importance in raising or lowering the value of districts, lands and estates; (4) it is unlawful to set a price on sacred acts on which divine institution has conferred a moral effect; this is the crime of simony. And it is immoral for a judge to put justice up for sale.

4. There are various reasons why the value of an object rises or falls, and why something may be preferred to another thing, though the latter seems to have equal or greater usefulness in human life. The primary factor is not the necessity of the thing or its surpassing usefulness; on the contrary we see that those things which are indispensable to human life are the cheapest, because by the singular providence of God nature pours out a plentiful supply of them.

The primary factor therefore in raising values is scarcity, whose effect is increased when things come from far away. Hence men's competitive luxury has put extraordinary value on many things which we could do without and still lead a commodious life, for example, pearls and jewels. And the value of things in daily use is particularly high when scarcity coincides with need or want. The values of man-made objects are most affected, apart from scarcity, by the subtlety and elegance of the art they display, sometimes too by the fame of the artist, the difficulty of the task, the scarcity of artists and workmen, and so on.

The value of services and actions is increased by their difficulty, the skill required, their usefulness and necessity; the scarcity of those who perform them, their social standing or free status; and finally, the actual reputation of the art, whether it is thought noble or ignoble. The opposite factors lower the values.

Finally, a particular object, though not generally valuable, is sometimes of great value to an individual, because of a special sentiment about it. It may be, for example, that it comes to us from a person who means much to us and was given to express his feelings, or that we have grown used to it; it may be a souvenir of some great event, or have helped us to avoid some great calamity; or perhaps we made it ourselves. This is called sentimental value.

5. Other factors are also normally taken into account in determining the values of particular things.

Among those who live together in a state of natural liberty, values are determined merely by agreement of the parties to the deal. For they are at liberty to alienate or acquire whatever they want, and they have no common master to regulate their dealings.

But in states the values of things are determined in two ways: (1) by the decree of a superior or by law; (2) by men's common valuation and assessment, or by the usage of the market together with the consent of those who are dealing with each other. Some like to call the former the legal price, the latter the common price.

When the legal price has been set in favour of the buyers (which is the usual case), sellers may not demand more, though they are not forbidden to accept less if they so wish. So when the rate of pay for services is publicly fixed in favour of employers, the workman may not demand more though he is not forbidden to take less.

6. But the common price, which is not set by law, has some latitude within which more or less may be and normally is offered and accepted, following the agreements of the parties doing business. It does however follow fairly clearly the usage of the market. For in the market account is normally taken of the labour and expense which the merchants are put to in transporting and handling their goods, as well as of how the item is bought or sold, whether in bulk or by retail. Sometimes too the common price suddenly changes because of a glut or a shortage of buyers, money or goods. For a shortage of buyers and money arising from a particular cause, together with an abundance of goods, lowers the price. By contrast, a glut of intending buyers, a large supply of money and a scarcity of goods raise the price. So too it makes for lower prices if goods are seeking a buyer. By contrast, the price rises when a seller who would otherwise not sell is approached by a buyer. Finally, one must also take into account whether one is offering cash or deferring payment, since time too is part of the price.

7. But after mankind had departed from its primitive simplicity and various forms of profit-making had come in, it was easily seen that the

common value alone was not adequate for handling the transactions men were engaged in and for the growth of commerce. For at that time commerce consisted in exchange alone and other people's services could only be hired by offering a service in return or handing over a piece of property. But after we began to desire so many different things for convenience or pleasure, it was obviously not easy for anyone to have at hand whatever another might want to take in exchange for his goods or which might be equivalent to them. And in civilized states where the citizens are distinguished by rank, it is necessary that there be several classes of men that could scarcely, if at all, maintain themselves, if a simple exchange of goods and services were in force. Hence most nations which had an ambition for an ampler way of life took the decision by agreement to endow one specific thing with eminent value, to which the common values of all other things would be related and in which they would be virtually contained. The consequence would be that by the mediation of that thing anyone could get for himself anything that was for sale and readily make all kinds of deals and contracts.

8. Most nations have chosen to use the nobler and rarer metals for this purpose. They are composed of highly durable substances, so that they are not easily worn by use and may be divided into many small pieces. They are equally convenient to store and to handle and their rarity makes them equal in value to many other things. Sometimes, however, by necessity and by lack of metals in certain countries, other things have been used instead of currency.

9. In states the sovereign has the right to establish the value of the currency; hence it is usually stamped with official symbols. In establishing the value of the currency we must take notice of the common valuation of neighbouring nations or trading partners. For otherwise if a state puts too high a value on its currency or if it does not mix the alloy properly, it will impede that part of its trade with its neighbours which cannot be conducted by simple exchange of goods. This is precisely the reason why a change in the value of the currency should not be made lightly, but only if required by a very severe crisis in the country. However, as the amount of gold and silver grows, automatically the value of the currency gradually decreases in relation ꞏ꞉ the price of land and of what depends on land.

15

On contracts which presuppose value in things and on the duties they involve

1. In its general sense an agreement [*pactum*] is the consent and concurrence of two or more men to the same intent [*placitum*]. But a distinction is often drawn between simple agreements and contracts [*contractus*], and the essence of the distinction seems to be that those agreements are called contracts which deal with things and actions of commercial significance and which consequently rest on a presupposition of ownership and value in things. Concurrence on other matters takes the common name of agreements, although to some of them the terms 'agreement' and 'contract' are applied indifferently.

2. Contracts may be divided into gratuitous and onerous. Gratuitous contracts confer a benefit on only one of the contracting parties, for example, mandate, loan for use, deposit. Onerous contracts bind both parties to an equal 'burden'; their characteristic is that something is given or some performance made for the purpose of getting the equivalent in return.

3. A requirement of all onerous contracts is that equality should prevail in them, or that both contracting parties receive equal benefit. Where inequality occurs, a right arises for the party which has received less to claim that his loss be made good, or simply to terminate the contract. This occurs particularly in states, since there the prices of things are determined by the custom of the market or by law. The essential requirement for discovering and determining this equality is that both contracting parties have knowledge of the thing which is the object of contract and of all its relevant qualities. Hence too in the process of passing a thing to another person by contract, one must point out its faults and defects as well as its good qualities.

Without this a fair price cannot be settled. However one does not need to point out circumstances which in themselves do not affect the thing, nor need one indicate faults which are known to both parties. Anyone who knowingly acquires a faulty object has only himself to blame.

4. The application of equality to these contracts is as follows. Although there may have been no dissimulation, if an inequality is discovered later, even without fault in the contracting parties (for example because the defect was latent or because there was a mistake in the price), the inequality must be corrected. Something must be taken from the party which profited and given to the party which suffered loss. However, to avoid a mass of litigation, the civil laws should give a remedy here only for extraordinary damage, and for the rest should tell everyone to look out for himself.

5. There are three important kinds of gratuitous contracts: mandate, loan for use, and deposit.

Mandate [*mandatum*] is when a person undertakes to manage another's business, without recompense, on his request and commission. This takes place in two ways: either he is instructed how he is to manage the business, or it is left to his own judgement and skill.

In this contract one must show the greatest good faith and diligence, since a person gives a mandate only to a friend of whom he has the highest opinion. Similarly, the party accepting the mandate must be indemnified for expenses incurred in the business entrusted to him, as well as for losses occasioned by the mandate and derived strictly from the business of the mandate.

6. Loan for use [*commodatum*] is the arrangement by which we allow someone the use of something which belongs to us.

Notice that one must keep and handle the object carefully and with the greatest diligence. One should not use it for other purposes, or further than the lender agreed. One should return it undamaged and as it was received, except for wear caused by normal use.

If the object was given for a fixed period, and if during that time the owner finds he has a great need of it, because something has happened which was unforeseen at the time of the loan, the object should be restored to him at his request without prevarication.

If the object of loan should perish by some unforeseen event or accident without any fault on the part of the borrower, one will not have to pay back its value if it would have perished anyway even had it remained in the owner's hands. If it would not have, it seems fair that the borrower should pay the value of the thing, since the owner would not have lost it but for his kindness to the other person. By the same token, the owner must refund any useful or necessary expenditure on the object of loan, apart from expenses normally attached to its use.

7. Deposit [*depositum*] is to entrust to another's good faith for safekeeping, without recompense, something that is ours or in some way concerns us.

The requirements are: that the thing entrusted must be diligently kept, and restored at the will of the depositor, unless restoration would be harmful to the owner or to others and should be put off for this reason. One may not use the object deposited without consent of the owner, if it would deteriorate in any way through use or if the owner's interest requires that it not be seen in public. If anyone takes the liberty of doing so, he will be liable for all the risks incurred in using it. He may also not remove the thing deposited from the bindings or boxes in which the depositor put it. It is highly shameful and worse than theft to refuse to return a deposit. It is yet more shameful to refuse to return a deposit of charity or anything deposited through risk of fire, collapse of a building or riot. For his part the depositor must refund expenses incurred in the deposit.

8. Perhaps the oldest of the onerous contracts is barter [*permutatio*]; it was the only means of commerce before the invention of money. In barter each side gives a thing for a thing of equal value. Even today, after the invention of money, there is a kind of barter especially common among traders, by which things are not compared directly with each other, but are first assessed in monetary terms and then exchanged for each other instead of for money.

Reciprocal donation is a different transaction from the contract of barter, in that there is no need to observe equality.

9. A sale [*emptio venditio*] is a transaction by which ownership of a thing or of a right equivalent to ownership is acquired for money.

The simplest kind of sale is when, after agreement on the price, the buyer immediately offers and delivers the price, and the seller offers and delivers the merchandise. However, it frequently happens that the merchandise is delivered immediately, but payment of the price is postponed for a fixed period. Sometimes the agreement on the price includes a condition that delivery of the thing, or merchandise, should be made by a certain date. In this case it is equitable that the thing should be at the seller's risk up to that date; but if after that date the buyer causes delay and hinders delivery of it, the risk for loss of it will then be the buyer's.

Various additional agreements may be added to a contract of sale. An example is provisional sale, by which the thing is sold subject to the seller's right to accept any better offer he may receive from anyone else by a certain date. There is also the forfeiture clause [*lex commissoria*], by which the sale is cancelled if the price is not paid by a certain day. There may also be a cancellation clause or agreement about return, and it may take three forms: either the buyer is obliged to restore the object to the seller, if the seller offers to return the purchase price (with or without certain time limitations); or, if the buyer offers to return the object, the seller is obliged to give back the purchase price; or, if the buyer wishes to sell it again himself, the previous seller must be allowed to buy it ahead of others: this is also called 'the right of first refusal'. In this connection, it is also common for the seller to reserve some small part of an estate sold or some particular use of it for himself.

There is also a kind of purchase, which they call buying a job lot, when many objects of different values are bought without piece by piece valuation but by an overall assessment, all lumped together, so to speak. In the kind of sale called 'auction', the object is knocked down to whichever of several bidders makes the best offer. Finally, there is a kind of purchase by which one buys not a definite object but only a likely expectation; an element of gambling is involved, so that neither party should complain – neither the buyer if his hopes are disappointed, nor the seller if the result is much above expectation.

10. Hire [*locatio conductio*] is an arrangement by which one makes over a service or the use of a thing to someone for payment.

It is normal to agree on the payment beforehand. However, if anyone offers a service or the use of something belonging to him without first settling the payment, he is taken to expect what common usage or the hirer's sense of fairness suggests.

One must notice the following about this contract. If a rented object is completely destroyed, from that moment the hirer is no longer obliged to pay the hire price or rent. In the case where the object rented (being something which has a definite use) suffers damage, the hirer subtracts from the rent the amount of usefulness it has lost, on the ground that the owner should supply it in a condition fit for use. In the case, however, that the yield of an object is not certain and contains an element of risk, a poor crop is the hirer's loss, just as an abundant crop is his gain. By strict right, nothing can be subtracted from the rent for a poor crop, especially since a poor crop in one year is normally followed by abundance in the next, unless the accidents which robbed him of the crop are quite uncommon and the hirer cannot be presumed to have taken on himself the risk that they would occur. Accidents of this kind should in all fairness justify reduction or remission of rent.

Just as the lessor of a property is obliged to ensure that it is ready for use and to bear all necessary expenses, so the lessee is bound to use it in the manner of a good householder and to make good anything lost by his own fault. Similarly, anyone who has contracted to perform a piece of work makes good anything damaged by his own fault.

One who has let out his services to do a temporary job cannot claim his pay when he is prevented by some accident from doing the job. But it is inhumane for an employer who has hired a man's services on a continuing basis either to dismiss him from his position or to make a deduction from his wages, if he is made incapable of work for a moderate period of time by sickness or other misfortune.

11. In the contract of loan for consumption [*mutuum*] a fungible thing is given to someone on the condition that after a certain period he return the same quantity and quality of the same kind of thing.

The objects of this sort of loan are called 'fungibles', or replaceable in their kind, because any object of that kind can replace any other, so that if one receives the same quantity and quality of the same kind of thing, one is said to have received the same as one gave. Things of this kind are determined and specified by weight, number and measure, and in this respect are normally referred to in terms of quantity rather than as specific items.

A loan is either a free loan, in which case one gets back no more than one gave, or a loan bringing profit, for which the term is 'interest' [*usura*]. There is nothing in this repugnant to natural law, provided that it is moderate and in line with the gain which the other party makes from the money or other object loaned and with the loss or lost profit which I incur by not having my property available; provided too that interest is not demanded from poor people, for whom a loan is a kind of charity.

12. In the contract of partnership [*societas*] two or more persons combine their money, property or services for the purpose of pro rata division between them of the profit it makes and similarly of a pro rata sharing between them of any loss that occurs.

In partnership, it is a matter of duty to show good faith and diligence, and one ought not to leave the partnership prematurely and in fraud of a partner.

On dissolution of a partnership, everyone receives what he contributed, with appropriate profit or loss. But if one partner has contributed money or goods, and the other has contributed services, it is necessary to look at the way the contribution has been made. For when the second party's services are limited to handling or retailing the money or goods of the first party, their respective shares of the profit have to correspond with the relation between the gain made on the money or goods and the value of the service; and the risk of loss of the capital lies wholly with the contributor. But when the service is devoted to improving the property which one party has contributed, the other party too is taken to have a share in it in proportion to the improvements he makes.

But when it is a partnership of the whole property of all the partners [*societas omnium bonorum*], individual partners must faithfully contribute the profits they make, and in return individuals are maintained from the common pool as their condition requires. And on dissolution of the partnership, a division of goods is made on the basis of what individuals brought into the partnership at the beginning. They do not ask whose goods were the source of their profit or loss (unless it was agreed otherwise).

13. There are several contracts which involve chance. Among these one may include bets, that is, when one party asserts and the other denies the occurrence of some result, not yet known to either party, and both deposit a certain sum which is to go to the party whose assertion is found to square with the result. Here belong games of every kind in which we play for something of value. Some of these have less of the character of gambling, since a contest of intelligence, dexterity, skill or strength is involved; in some, intelligence and luck have equal scope, while in others luck predominates. It is for the government of the country to determine how far it is in the public interest or that of individuals to tolerate this kind of contract. Here too belong lotteries: that is, when several persons contribute money to

buy an object and then determine by lot to whom the whole thing is to go; likewise the raffle, in which a certain number of tallies or tickets, some inscribed, some blank, are thrown into a vase, and a person pays for the right of picking one and gets what is written on the ticket. Insurance is akin to these contracts. It is a contract for avoiding risk and repairing its effects, by which for a certain sum of money someone undertakes to be liable for the risks which goods are likely to suffer in transport from one place to another; so that if they happen to perish, the insurer is obliged to pay the owner their value.

14. Suretyships and pledges are frequently employed to lend more strength and security to contracts.

In suretyship [*fidejussio*], a third party, acceptable to the creditor, takes on himself the obligation of the principal debtor as a kind of reserve, so that if the debtor fails to pay, he takes his place; the condition is that the principal debtor must refund his expenditure.

A surety cannot be made liable for a greater sum than the principal debtor. Nevertheless, he may be more strictly obliged than the debtor, since more reliance is placed on him than on the debtor. Naturally, however, the principal debtor is to be called upon before the surety, unless the latter has taken the debtor's obligation entirely upon himself, and in this case he is normally called a 'new debtor' [*expromissor*].

If several persons go surety for one, each is to be called upon only pro rata, unless one of them is not in a position to pay or there is no chance of calling upon him. In this case the remainder are burdened with his share.

15. The other frequent form of security for a loan is that something belonging to the debtor is delivered or assigned to the creditor under the name of pledge or mortgage, until the debt is paid off. The purpose of this is both to put pressure on the debtor to pay because he wants to recover his property, and to make available to the creditor a source of payment. Hence pledges are normally of equal or greater value than the actual debt.

Objects put up as pledges are either productive or unproductive. In the first case, it is normal to add an agreement about use of the pledge [*antichresis*], so that the creditor may collect the product of the pledge as a kind of interest. If the pledge is not productive, the law on forfeiture applies, that is, the pledge goes to the creditor if payment is not made within a certain time. This is not by nature unjust provided that the pledge is not worth more than the debt together with interest accruing during the period, or that the surplus is given back to the owner.

A creditor must give back the pledge when payment is made. Therefore during the intervening period he owes it no less care than he gives to his own property; and where no contract of '*antichresis*' has been made, and it is the kind of object that wears out with use, or if there is any effect at all on the debtor's interest, the creditor may not use it without the debtor's permission.

A mortgage differs from a pledge in that whereas a pledge involves the delivery of the thing, a mortgage consists simply in the bare assignment of a piece of property and particularly of an immovable, from which the creditor may recover his loan if payment is not forthcoming.

16. The duties of the contracting parties are clearly apparent from the nature and purpose of these contracts.

16

On methods of dissolving obligations arising from agreements

1. There are various methods of dissolving obligations based on agreement the effect of which is the extinction of the duties derived from them. The most natural is the fulfilment or payment of what was agreed upon. It is normally the debtor who is obliged to pay; but the obligation is also dissolved if performance is made by another party in the name of the person who contracted the obligation, if in fact it would not make any difference who satisfies the agreement. There is a condition, however, that the person who pays for another without the intention of making it a gift may claim from him what he has spent.

Payment must be made to the creditor, or to one whom he has delegated to accept the debt in his name.

Finally, performance or payment must be exactly what was agreed upon, not something else instead; it must be whole, not damaged, not merely a part and not divided; and it must be at the time and place agreed. However, the creditor's humanity or the debtor's inability to pay may often force an extension of the payment date or acceptance of something else instead.

2. Obligations are also extinguished by compensation. This is a reciprocal adjustment of credit and debt, or the liberation of the debtor for the reason that the creditor evidently owes him in his turn something of the same kind and value. For 'so much' is 'the same', particularly in the case of fungibles, and in the case of a reciprocal debt I would have to give straight back what I have just received. Therefore to avoid unnecessary transactions the most convenient way of making the payment is for both parties to keep what they have.

It is obvious that compensation in the strict sense is properly made where it is a question of fungible objects of the same kind whether at the due time for payment or later, but not where it is a question of other things or other types of performance, unless on both sides they are reduced to an estimate of their value, that is to money.

3. An obligation is also ended by release, or remission offered by the person to whom the debt was due and who had an interest in the fulfilment of the obligation. Release may be given explicitly by use of signs indicating consent, for example, by giving a formal discharge or by returning or destroying the deeds of loan. It may also be given tacitly by directly preventing payment or by causing such prevention.

4. Obligations which require performance by both parties are normally dissolved by mutual withdrawal from the agreement before any performance has been made on the contract, unless the laws of the land forbid it. But if either party has made some performance, he must either provide a release or be compensated in some other way.

5. Breach of faith by either party breaks rather than dissolves the obligation. When one party does not carry through his side of the agreement, the other party is not bound to perform what he undertook in expectation of the other's performance. For the later items in agreements are conditional upon performance of the earlier items, as if the wording were: 'I will perform, if you perform first.'

6. Obligations also expire when either party – the subject of its obligation or its due recipient – changes the state of affairs which was the sole ground of the obligation.

7. Obligations whose duration is set by a date expire simply through the running out of time, unless extended by express or tacit agreement by the parties. The opportunity must have existed within that period to complete the obligation.

8. Finally, obligations essentially rooted in a man's person are dissolved by death. Remove the subject, and the accidents too are necessarily extinguished. Often, however, the obligations of the dead do continue in the survivors. This happens either because a survivor takes it upon himself to fulfil the obligations of the deceased as a duty of family piety or for other reasons, or because he must satisfy an obligation from the estate of the deceased which has come to him as heir with this encumbrance.

9. By delegation I offer to my creditor, with his consent, someone who owes me a debt, as a substitute who will pay my debt to my

creditor for me. Here the consent of the creditor is required but not that of the third party debtor, who may not even know that I have delegated my debt to him and would refuse if he did know, so long as the creditor accepts it. For it makes no difference to the debtor which one of us he pays, but it does make a great difference to the creditor whether he is to claim his debt from me or from the other.

17
On interpretation

1. It is certainly true that one's obligation in matters enjoined by authority is limited to what the authority intended, just as one's own voluntary commitments extend no further than one's intention. But a man cannot tell another man's will except from acts and signs apparent to his senses. Hence one's obligations, so far as human judgement goes, are held to consist in what a correct interpretation of the signs indicates. It is therefore a great contribution to a proper understanding of laws and agreements, and of doing one's duty on the basis of them, to draw up rules of sound interpretation, and particularly the interpretation of words, since words are the commonest signs.
2. The rule about words in common use is: words are normally to be taken in their own proper and accepted sense, the sense which they have not so much from strict propriety or grammatical analogy or similarity of derivation as from common usage. 'Common usage is the arbiter, the law and the norm of speech.'[1]
3. Terms of art are to be explained according to the definitions of the experts in each art. But if terms of art are differently defined by different experts, it will tend to avoid disputes if we express in ordinary words what we understand by any particular term.
4. Conjectures are needed to extract the real meaning, if words or expressions are ambiguous, or if certain parts of a piece seem to contradict each other, provided that they can be reconciled by skilful exegesis. For where there is a certain and obvious contradiction, the later passage supersedes the earlier.

---

[1] Horace, *Ars poetica*, 72.

5. Conjectures about the intention and correct sense of an ambiguous or intricate passage are made on the basis of subject-matter, effect and related passages.

The rule on subject-matter is: words are normally to be understood in the light of the subject. For the speaker is presumed always to have in mind the subject of his discourse; and therefore the meanings of the words should always be appropriate to it.

6. The rule on effect and consequences is: if the words taken in a simple, literal sense would have no effect or an absurd effect, one should diverge from the commonly accepted sense only so far as is necessary to avoid meaninglessness or absurdity.

7. The most valid conjectures are derived from related passages, because a person is normally assumed to be consistent. Passages may be related either in place or merely in source. The rule on the former is: if the sense is made plain and clear in some passage of the same work, the more obscure expressions should be interpreted in the light of plain expressions. A second related rule is: in interpreting any passage, careful attention must be paid to the preceding and following passages; the assumption is that the passage that comes between them fits and agrees. The rule on passages from the same source is: within an author's works an obscure expression should be interpreted in the light of his own clearer expressions, even if they were published at a different time and place, unless it is obvious that he has changed his mind.

8. It is also valuable in uncovering the true sense, especially in interpreting laws, to look at the reason for the law [*ratio legis*], or the cause and consideration that moved the legislator to bring it in, especially when it is clear that it was the only reason for the law. The rule here is: follow the interpretation of the law which agrees with the reason for the law and reject that which is inconsistent with it. Likewise, when the sole, sufficient reason for the law ceases to exist, the law also ceases. But when there was more than one reason for the law, the whole law does not cease if one reason ceases to exist, since the rest may be sufficient to maintain it. Often too the legislator's will by itself is enough, however unapparent to his subjects the reason for the law may be.

9. Note too that many words have more than one sense, a broader and a stricter. And again the substance may be favourable, invidious or mixed. It is favourable if it protects equality in the position of both

parties, if it seeks the common interest or lends support to legislative acts, if it promotes peace, and so on. It is invidious if it is to the detriment of one party only or of one party more than another, if it carries with it a penalty, or subverts an act, or changes the status quo, or promotes war. It is mixed if, for example, it changes the status quo, but for the sake of peace.

The rule here is: interpret favourable expressions more broadly, invidious expressions more strictly.

10. There are also conjectures of other than verbal origin, which cause the interpretation sometimes to be broadened, sometimes to be narrowed, though it is easier to find reasons to suggest a narrower than a broader interpretation.

A law, then, may be broadened to include a case which is not made explicit in it, if it is clear that the reason which fits the present case was the legislator's only reason, and that he took it in its widest extent, intending, in particular, to include equivalent cases. A law should also be extended to deal with cases which are devised by cunning men of wicked ingenuity to get around the law.

11. Restriction on words framed in general terms occurs either from an original defect of intention or from a conflict between a new case and that intention. One understands that something may be presumed not to have been in the original intention of the legislator: (1) from the absurdity which would otherwise follow, where no sane man (it is thought) would have had this intention; hence general terms must be taken in a stricter sense in cases where otherwise an absurdity would result; (2) from the absence of the sole reason which informed his intention; hence cases which do not square with the sole and sufficient reason for the law are not comprehended in a general expression; (3) from the absence of the subject which the speaker is thought to have had constantly in mind; hence general terms must always be taken in a sense appropriate to the subject.

12. A conflict between the will of the legislator and subsequently emerging cases is discovered either by natural reason or from some indication of his will.

It is discovered by natural reason if it would be inconsistent with equity if certain cases were not exempted from the general law. For equity is the correction of what is deficient in the law because of its universality. Because of the infinite variety of possible cases, not all can be foreseen or expressed, and therefore when general words have to be applied to special cases, one must exempt those which the legislator would have exempted himself if he had been consulted on such a case. However, one may not have recourse to equity without the force of adequate signs. The surest of them is if it is apparent that natural law would be violated if one followed closely the letter of human law. The second most convincing sign is the situation where, though it is not forbidden to follow the letter of the law, still to the eye of humanity it would seem oppressive and intolerable (whether for all men generally or for particular persons), or the situation where the purpose of the law would seem too dearly achieved at the price.

13. Finally, one must also allow an exception to a general expression, if the wording of another passage elsewhere and the law or agreement in question cannot both be observed in the present circumstances, even if there is no formal conflict.

Certain rules need to be observed here, to understand which law should be followed in the case where both cannot be followed at the same time. (1) What is merely permitted gives way to an order. (2) What must be done at a certain time takes precedence over what can be done at any time. (3) An affirmative precept gives way to a negative precept; or when an affirmative precept cannot be obeyed without violating a negative precept, one should decline to follow it for the time being. (4) Where agreements and laws are equal in other respects, prefer the particular to the general. (5) If at a certain point in time the performance of two duties conflicts, it is reasonable to give precedence to the one which can be justified as the better or more useful of the two. (6) A sworn agreement takes precedence over an unsworn agreement when both cannot be fulfilled at the same time. (7) An imperfect obligation gives way to a perfect obligation. (8) A law of beneficence gives way, all things being equal, to a law of gratitude.

Samuel Pufendorf

ON THE DUTY OF MAN AND CITIZEN ACCORDING TO NATURAL LAW

BOOK II

I
On men's natural state

1. We must next inquire into the duties which fall to man to perform as a result of the different states in which we find him existing in social life. By 'state' [*status*] in general, we mean a condition in which men are understood to be set for the purpose of performing a certain class of actions. Each state also has its own distinctive laws [*jura*].

2. Men's state is either natural or adventitious. Natural state may be considered, in the light of reason alone, in three ways: in relation to God the Creator; or in the relation of each individual man to himself; or in relation to other men.

3. Considered from the first point of view, the natural state of man is the condition in which he was placed by his Creator with the intention that he be an animal excelling other animals. It follows from this state that man should recognize and worship his Creator, admire His works, and lead his life in a manner utterly different from that of the animals. Hence this state is in complete contrast with the life and condition of the animals.

4. From the second point of view, we may consider the natural state of man, by an imaginative effort, as the condition man would have been in if he had been left to himself alone, without any support from other men, given the condition of human nature as we now perceive it. It would have been, it seems, more miserable than that of any beast, if we reflect on the great weakness of man as he comes into this world, when he would straight away die without help from others, and on the primitive life he would lead if he had no other resources than he owes to his own strength and intelligence. One may put it more strongly: the fact that we have been able to grow out of such weakness, the fact

that we now enjoy innumerable good things, the fact that we have cultivated our minds and bodies for our own and others' benefit – all this is the result of help from others. In this sense the natural state is opposed to life improved by human industry.

5. From the third point of view, we consider the natural state of man in terms of the relationship which men are understood to have with each other on the basis of the simple common kinship which results from similarity of nature and is antecedent to any agreement or human action by which particular obligations of one to another have arisen. In this sense men are said to live in a natural state with each other when they have no common master, when no one is subject to another and when they have no experience either of benefit or of injury from each other. In this sense the natural state is opposed to the civil state.

6. The character of the natural state, furthermore, may be considered either as it is represented by fiction or as it is in reality. It would be a fiction if we supposed that in the beginning there existed a multitude of men without any dependence on each other, as in the myth of the brothers of Cadmus,[1] or if we imagined that the whole human race was so widely scattered that every man governed himself separately, and the only bond between them was likeness of nature. But the natural state which actually exists shows each man joined with a number of other men in a particular association, though having nothing in common with all the rest except the quality of being human and having no duty to them on any other ground. This is the condition [*status*] that now exists between different states [*civitas*] and between citizens of different countries [*respublica*], and which formerly obtained between heads of separate families.

7. Indeed it is obvious that the whole human race was never at one and the same time in the natural state. The children of our first parents, from whom the Holy Scriptures teach that all mortal men take their origin, were subject to the same paternal authority [*patria potestas*]. Nevertheless, the natural state emerged among certain men later. For the earliest men sought to fill the empty world and to find more ample living space for themselves and their cattle, and so left the paternal home scattering in different directions; and individual males established their own families. Their descendants dispersed in the

---

[1] Phoenix and Cilix, eponymous ancestors of, respectively, the Phoenicians and the Cilicians.

same way, and the special bond of kinship, and the affection that goes with it, gradually withered away leaving only that common element that results from similarity of nature. The human race then multiplied remarkably; men recognized the disadvantages of life apart; and gradually, those who lived close to each other drew together, at first in small states [*civitates*], then in larger states as the smaller coalesced, freely or by force. Among these states the natural state [*status*] still certainly exists; their only bond is their common humanity.

8. The principal law of those who live in the natural state is to be subject only to God and answerable to none but Him. In that respect this state has the name of natural liberty. By natural liberty every man is understood to be in his own right and power and not subject to anyone's authority without a preceding human act. This is also the reason why every man is held to be equal to every other, where there is no relationship of subjection.

Since, moreover, men have the light of reason implanted in them to govern their actions by its illumination, it follows that someone living in natural liberty does not depend on anyone else to rule his actions, but has the authority to do anything that is consistent with sound reason by his own judgement and at his own discretion. And owing to the inclination which a man shares with all living things, he must infallibly and by all means strive to preserve his body and life and to repel all that threatens to destroy them, and take measures necessary to that end; and since in the natural state no one has a superior to whom he has subjected his will and judgement, everyone decides for himself whether the measures are apt to conduce to self-preservation or not. For no matter how attentively he listens to the advice of others, it is still up to him whether he will take it or not. It is, however, essential that he conduct his government of himself, if it is to go well, by the dictates of right reason and natural law.

9. The state of nature may seem extraordinarily attractive in promising liberty and freedom from all subjection. But in fact before men submit to living in states, it is attended with a multitude of disadvantages, whether we imagine individuals existing in that state or consider the condition of separate heads of households. For if you picture to yourself a person (even an adult) left alone in this world without any of the aids and conveniences by which human ingenuity has relieved and enriched our lives, you will see a naked dumb animal, without resources, seeking to satisfy his hunger with roots and grasses and his

thirst with whatever water he can find, to shelter himself from the inclemencies of the weather in caves, at the mercy of wild beasts, fearful of every chance encounter. Those who were members of scattered families may have enjoyed a somewhat more developed way of life but in no way comparable with civil life; and this not so much because of poverty, which the family (where desires are limited) seems capable of relieving, as because it can do little to ensure security. To put the matter in a few words, in the state of nature each is protected only by his own strength; in the state by the strength of all. There no one may be sure of the fruit of his industry; here all may be. There is the reign of the passions, there there is war, fear, poverty, nastiness, solitude, barbarity, ignorance, savagery; here is the reign of reason, here there is peace, security, wealth, splendour, society, taste, knowledge, benevolence.

10. In the natural state, if one does not do for another what is due by agreement, or does him wrong, or if a dispute arises in other ways, there is no one who can by authority compel the offender to perform his part of the agreement or make restitution, as is possible in states, where one may implore the aid of a common judge. But as nature does not allow one to plunge into war on the slightest provocation, even when one is fully convinced of the justice of his cause, an attempt must first be made to settle the matter by gentler means, namely, by friendly discussion between the parties and an absolute (not conditional) mutual promise or by appeal to the decision of arbitrators.

Such arbitrators must be fair to both sides and not show prejudice or favour in giving their verdict; they must look only at the merits of the case. For the same reason a man is not appointed as arbitrator in a case in which he has greater expectation of benefit or glory from the victory of one of the parties than from the other, and so has an interest in one party winning the case no matter how. So there must be no agreement or promise between the arbitrator and the parties, to oblige him to pronounce in favour of one rather than the other.

If the arbitrator cannot ascertain the state of the facts either from the common admissions of the parties or on the basis of reliable documents or of arguments and evidence that admit no doubt, the facts will have to be ascertained from statements by witnesses. Natural law, and in many cases the sanctity of an oath, constrain witnesses to tell the truth; but it would be safest not to accept as witnesses those who have such feelings about either of the parties that their conscience must struggle so to speak with friendship, hatred, vindictiveness or some other strong emotional impulse, or even with some more intimate bond; not everybody has sufficient firmness to overcome these feelings. Sometimes litigation may be avoided by the mediation of mutual friends, which is rightly considered to be among the most sacred duties. But in the natural state, the individual is responsible for execution of the judgement, when one party will not voluntarily render what is due.

11. Nature herself has willed that there should be a kind of kinship among men, by force of which it is wrong to harm another man and indeed right for everyone to work for the benefit of others. However, kinship usually has a rather weak force among those who live in natural liberty with each other. Consequently, we have to regard any man who is not our fellow-citizen, or with whom we live in a state of nature, not indeed as our enemy, but as a friend we cannot wholly rely on. The reason is that men not only can do each other very great harm, but do very often wish to do so for various reasons. Some are driven to injure others by their wickedness of character, or by lust for power and superfluous wealth. Others, though men of moderation, take up arms to preserve themselves and not to be forestalled by others. Many find themselves in conflict because they are competing for the same object, others through rivalry of talents. Hence in the natural state there is a lively and all but perpetual play of suspicion, distrust, eagerness to subvert the strength of others, and desire to get ahead of them or to augment one's own strength by their ruin. Therefore as a good man should be content with his own and not trouble others or covet their goods, so a cautious man who loves his own security will believe all men his friends but liable at any time to become enemies; he will keep peace with all, knowing that it may soon be exchanged for war. This is the reason why that country is considered happy which even in peace contemplates war.

2

On the duties of marriage

1. The first of the adventitious states in which a man is set by some prior human act is marriage. Marriage may be called the first example of social life and at the same time the seed-bed of the human race. 2. And first of all it is a settled point that the burning attraction of the sexes to each other has not been designed by the Creator in His great wisdom for the satisfaction of empty pleasure; for taken by itself it was bound to generate extreme nastiness and disorder in the human race. But it has been given to enhance relations between man and wife and to encourage them to put themselves to the trouble of having children and of bearing the difficulties which attend their birth and upbringing.

It follows from this that any employment of the genital members which deviates from these purposes is repugnant to natural law. Under this heading come forbidden lust directed towards a different species or towards persons of the same sex; any kind of filthy impurity; and all extra-marital intercourse, whether by mutual consent or against the woman's will.

3. The obligation to contract marriage may be considered either with respect to the human race as a whole or with respect to individuals.

In the first respect the obligation is that the propagation of the human race must absolutely not proceed by way of casual and promiscuous intercourse. It should always be bound by the laws of matrimony and therefore only practised within marriage. Without this a decent and well-ordered society among men and the development of civil life are inconceivable.

In the second respect individuals are obliged to enter into marriage

when a suitable opportunity occurs. This is determined not only by age and the capacity to beget, but also by the chance of a suitable match and the capacity to support the wife and any children there may be; also by whether the man is fit to take on the role of head of the family. An exception is made for anyone who has the temperament to lead a chaste life as a single person, and feels that he can achieve more good for the human race or for his country by not marrying than by marrying, especially when there is no fear of a shortage of children.
4. There usually is, and always should be, an agreement made between those who are about to enter into matrimony. A regular and complete agreement will consist of the following articles:

(1) It is appropriate to the character of both sexes that the contract should be initiated by the man. Since the man's purpose surely is to have children of his own – not supposititious children or children of adultery – the woman should solemnly promise to the man that she will not grant the use of her body to anyone except him. In return the wife usually receives the same solemn promise from the husband.

(2) Nothing is more incompatible with the character of social and civil life than a casual and vagabond way of life, with no fixed abode and no settled property. The most advantageous way of bringing up a child (who belongs to both the parents) is by their combined efforts. Moreover, living together without interruption is a great joy for couples who are well-suited and also gives the husband greater assurance of his wife's fidelity. For all these reasons a wife gives her husband this further promise to live with him without interruption and to make the closest association of their lives together and form one family. Implicit in this is a mutual promise that they will behave to each other as the nature of this association requires.

(3) It is particularly in keeping with the natural condition of both sexes not only that the man's position should be superior, but also that the husband should be the head of the family which he has established. It follows that the wife should be liable to the direction of her husband in matters concerning the marriage and the household. Hence it is for the husband to decide where they will live, and the wife may not go away against his will or sleep apart from him. It does not, however, seem necessary to the

essence of marriage that his authority should include the right of life and death, severe punishment, or full power to dispose of any or all of the wife's property, though such authority is established in some places by particular agreement between the spouses or by the civil laws.

5. Though it is plainly against natural law that one woman should live at the same time with more than one man, it has been the custom among very many peoples, including formerly the Jewish people itself, that one man may have two or more wives at the same time. Nevertheless, even apart from the original institution of marriage as related in Holy Scripture, it is established on the basis of right reason itself that it is much more appropriate as well as more useful that one man be content with one woman. And this has been the custom approved among all the Christian nations that we know of these many centuries.

6. The close nature of this union indicates no less clearly that marriage should be perpetual, to be terminated only by the death of one of the spouses, unless the terms of the original marriage agreement have been violated by adultery or wilful desertion. In the case of incompatibility of character which does not have the same effect as wilful desertion, simple separation as to bed and board is the accepted custom among Christians, without permission to make a second set of marriage vows. One of the reasons for this is to prevent the capacity for divorce from encouraging wilful immorality, and to give an incentive to spouses to be flexible and tolerant of each other, because they have no hope of a second marriage. However if the terms of the marriage contract have been broken, the injured party alone is released from the bond; the bond remains in force for the other party, in case the injured party may desire to be reconciled and deigns to do so.

7. Any man can legitimately contract a marriage with any woman where the civil law poses no obstacle, if the age and physical condition appropriate to marriage are present, unless an obstacle exists in the form of a moral impediment. There is a moral impediment against either a man or a woman taking another spouse if either of them already has a spouse.

8. Another factor held to be a moral impediment to legal marriage is too close a relationship of blood or affinity. This is the reason why natural law, too, considers marriages between ascendants and

descendants, however far apart, to be sinful. Marriages on the transverse line, for example with an aunt on either side, or with a sister, and likewise, in terms of affinity, with a stepmother, mother-in-law or stepdaughter, are abominated not only by divine law but also by the laws of civilized nations and the consensus of Christians. Moreover, the civil laws of many peoples have banned certain more remote degrees, in order to throw as it were a hedge around the more solemn degrees previously mentioned, so that there would be some barrier to easy violation of them.

9. In other contracts and transactions the civil laws have normally added certain definite requirements, lack of observance of which destroys their validity in a civil court. So it is in the case of marriage, in that certain solemnities are required by the civil laws in some places for the sake of decency and good order. Though these things are outside the scope of natural law, those who are subject to civil laws will not contract a legal marriage without them; or at least a union of that kind will not have the same effects in the state as a regular marriage.

10. The duty of a husband is to love, support, govern and protect his wife; of a wife to love and honour her husband, and to be a helpmate to him, not only in bearing and raising children, but also in taking upon herself some of the concerns of the household. On both sides the close character of the union requires the spouses to be partners in good and bad fortune alike, and if either is struck by disaster, the other is obliged to give support. Each should also show common sense and temper their behaviour to preserve mutual harmony, though in this role it is more for the wife to give way.

3
On the duties of parents and children

1. The issue of marriage is children; paternal power [*patria potestas*] has been established over them. It is the oldest as well as the most sacred form of authority [*imperium*]. It binds children to respect the orders of parents and to acknowledge their preeminence over themselves.

2. Parents' authority over children has its origin in two chief causes. The first is that the natural law itself, in commanding men to be sociable, imposes on parents a care for their children. To prevent negligence, nature has implanted in parents a most tender affection for them. Exercise of that care requires the power [*potestas*] to direct the children's actions for their own security, which they do not yet discern for themselves since they lack judgement.

Secondly, this authority rests also on the tacit consent of the child. One may rightly assume that if the infant had had the use of reason at the time of birth, and had been able to perceive that he could not survive without his parents' care and the government implied by that care, he would gladly have agreed to it, and stipulated in return that they give him a good upbringing. In practice parents' authority over children is established when they acknowledge them, feed them and undertake to shape them into good members of human society.

3. The mother contributes as much as the father to the generation of a child and so in a physical sense the offspring belongs equally to both of them. One must therefore inquire carefully which has the superior right to the child.

Here one must make a clear distinction. If the child was conceived outside of marriage, it will belong primarily to the mother. The reason is that the father can only be identified by the mother's testimony.

Those, too, who live in natural liberty or above the civil laws may make an agreement that it is the mother's right, not the father's, that prevails.

But in states – and states have certainly been formed by men, not women – the right of the father will prevail, since a contract of marriage normally originates with the man and he becomes the head of the family. Consequently, though children certainly owe their mother respect and gratitude, they need not obey her orders if these conflict with reasonable instructions from their father. However, if the father dies, his right over the children, at least until they are adult, seems to accrue to the mother; and if she enters a second marriage, it passes to the stepfather, since he takes over the responsibility and the concern of the natural parent. And when someone undertakes to raise as a free man a child who has been abandoned or orphaned, he may (in his own right) insist upon filial obedience from him.

4. For a more precise understanding of the extent of parents' power over their children, one must distinguish among heads of households between those who live independently of each other and those who have submitted to a state, and between the authority a father has as such and the power he has as head of his household.

Nature has imposed a duty upon a father to bring up his children properly so that they may turn out to be good members of human society. Hence a father is permitted the power necessary for this purpose. But this power certainly does not go so far as to permit parents to abort the embryo in the mother's womb or to abandon and kill the new-born. For though it is true that the offspring is of the substance of the parents, still it shares the same human condition as the parents and is capable of being wronged by them. Nor does this parental authority seem to extend as far as to the exercise of the right of life and death for wrongdoing, but is limited to reasonable chastisement. For we are dealing with a tender age, when such atrocious crimes as merit expiation by death scarcely occur. Nevertheless, if a boy pertinaciously rejects all discipline, and there is no hope of improvement, he may be expelled from his father's house and disowned.

5. Parental power in this limited sense may be considered next in terms of the different stages of a child's development.

At the first stage, when the use of reason is still undeveloped, all children's actions are subject to the control of parents. If at this stage any property is transferred by others to the minor, it should be accepted and administered by the father for the son, though the ownership goes to the son; but it is reasonable that the profits should fall to the father until the son reaches maturity. Similarly the father rightly claims for himself whatever gain or emolument results from the son's labour and must for his part provide for his nurture and upbringing.

6. When the children in adult years are endowed with mature judgement but still form part of the paternal family, one must consider separately the authority which a father has as begetter and that which he has as head of the family. Since in the former case he has as his aim the proper raising and discipline of the children, it is clear that grown children too should follow the guidance of their parents as wiser than themselves.

And whoever wishes to be maintained from his father's property and later to succeed to it should accommodate himself to the ways of the father's house, the governance of which is in any case the father's privilege.

7. But heads of households before they entered into states had exercised in their homes a sort of princely authority. Hence while the children remained in their households, they had a duty to regard their fathers' authority as supreme.

But afterwards household authority (along with other rights) was adapted to the use and style of the state; and in some places much authority, in others little, was left to the fathers. Hence we see that in some states fathers have had the right of life and death over their children, to be exercised in cases of wrongdoing, but in others that right was taken from them, for fear that they would misuse their power to the detriment of the public good and the wicked abuse of their children; and so that their children's vices would not be indulgently overlooked by paternal affection and later erupt and cause public disaster; and to relieve fathers from the obligation of pronouncing so harsh a sentence.

8. But when the child has left his father's house for good, and has set up a new household of his own or joined another, the father's power is dissolved. The debt of gratitude and respect remains, however, because it is founded in the parents' deserts, which, it is generally believed, children never or very rarely requite. Those deserts consist partly of children's owing their life to their parents, which is the *sine*

qua non of all their blessings. The parents also undertook the laborious and expensive task of bringing them up and making them fit members of human society, and have given them the means to lead comfortable and prosperous lives.

9. Although nature lays the obligation of raising children on the parents, this is no bar to delegating the execution of the task to someone else, if it is necessary or to the child's advantage. However, the parent does reserve to himself the right of supervising the delegate.

This justifies a father in entrusting the instruction of his son to suitable teachers. It also justifies his giving his son for adoption if the son is likely to derive some profit from it.

And if there is no other means of supporting his child, a father may give up his son as a pledge for a loan, or sell him into endurable slavery rather than let him die of want, at least on the condition that these acts may be revoked, when the father achieves a better fortune or a relative is willing to buy back the child. However, if a parent exposes and abandons the child from sheer inhumanity, whoever takes him up and raises him also succeeds to the father's rights, so that the foster-child owes filial obedience to the person who is bringing him up.

10. A father should not expel a child from his household, while it still needs to be helped and brought up, without the gravest reasons. Likewise, a child should not leave his father's household without the father's permission. Now, it is usually on the occasion of marriage that children leave their father's household, and it is in any case a matter of importance to the parents whom their child is to marry and from whom their grandchildren will be born. Consequently, a child's filial duty plainly requires that children obtain their father's consent in this matter and not take a spouse against his will. However, if children have in fact contracted and consummated a marriage against their parents' will, it seems that it is not invalid by natural law, especially when they do not intend to be a burden on the father's household any longer and the match is not unsuitable in other ways. Hence, if in some places such marriages are held to be invalid or unlawful, that is a matter of the civil laws.

11. The duty of parents consists principally of properly supporting their children, of forming body and mind by an appropriate and intelligent upbringing, so that they become decent and useful mem-

bers of human and civil society, honest, intelligent and of good character. They should also put them in the way of a suitable and honest occupation, and establish and advance their fortune so far as means and opportunity allow.

12. The duty of children, on the other hand, is to honour their parents, that is, to show respect for them not only by outward signs but much more in their own inner valuation of them, as authors of their life and of so many other benefits; to obey them; to take care of them, so far as they can, especially in need or old age; to do nothing of great importance without their advice and authority; and finally to bear patiently with any fretfulness or faults they find in them.

4
On the duties of masters and slaves[1]

1. After the human race had begun to multiply, and the advantage had been realized of having one's domestic affairs looked after by the service of others, the custom was early introduced of admitting slaves [*servus*] to one's household to perform the required labours. In the beginning slaves probably offered themselves of their own free will; their motive was poverty, or a sense of their own lack of intelligence. They committed their services to the master in perpetuity, stipulating for a perennial provision to themselves of food and other necessities. Subsequently, as wars everywhere became more frequent, most peoples adopted the custom that prisoners of war in return for their lives be taken into servitude together with any offspring they might subsequently have. However, many peoples have no servitude of this kind in current use, but have all their household tasks performed by wage-earners hired for a period.

2. As there are different degrees of servitude, so the power of masters and the condition of the servants vary.

A temporary wage-earner is owed an agreed wage by his master, and owes him in return an agreed service. In this contract the master has the superior standing; and so an assistant of this kind is obliged to show respect to the master in proportion to the latter's dignity; he is liable to punishment when he does his work badly or negligently, but it should not go so far as to inflict serious physical injury and much less death on the master's own authority.

3. The kind of servant who has bound himself to someone of his own

---

[1] '*Servus*': Pufendorf uses this term to cover both 'servant' and 'slave'.

free will for perpetual servitude is owed by his master food and the other necessities of life for ever. In return he has to do whatever services the master requires and faithfully account to the master for whatever profits he makes. In all this, however, the master will have a humane regard for the slave's strength and skill and will not brutally insist on labour that exceeds his strength. He is subject also to the master's correction, in the sense not only of putting an end to negligence in doing his work, but also of conforming his manners to the dignity and tranquillity of the household. However, such a slave may not be sold to another against his will because he voluntarily chose this master, not another one; and it matters to him whom he serves. If he commits a serious crime against a person outside the family, he is subject, in states, to the penalty of the civil power; where the household lives separately, he may be expelled from it. But when the crime is against a separate household itself, he may be given even the extreme penalty.

4. Slaves captured in war were usually treated quite harshly at first because something of the anger one feels towards an enemy was still felt against them, and because they had themselves made an extreme attack upon ourselves and our fortunes. However, as soon as a mutual agreement of association in the household has been made between victor and vanquished, all past enmity is deemed to be remitted. After that it is a wrong on the part of the master even in the case of a slave so acquired either to fail to provide him with the necessities of life or to be harsh to him without reason, much less to put him to death, unless he has committed a capital crime.

5. In the case of slaves who had been reduced to that condition by the violence of war, as well as those who had been bought, it was the custom that they might be transferred to whomever we pleased, just like our other property, and be put up for sale in the manner of merchandise; the slave's actual body was understood to belong to the master. But since humanity bids us never to forget that a slave is in any case a man, we should by no means treat him like other property, which we may use, abuse and destroy at our pleasure.[2] And when one decides to transfer to another a slave of this kind, one should take even more pains than the slave deserves to ensure that he is not sent somewhere where he will be treated inhumanely.

---

[2] *Cf.* the Romanist definition of ownership as '*jus utendi fruendi abutendi*'.

6. Finally, a point everywhere recognized: the offspring of slave parents is itself of servile status, and belongs, as a piece of property, to the owner of the mother. This practice is defended by the argument that it is reasonable that the product that issues from the body should belong to the body's owner; and because that offspring would obviously not have been born if the master had exercised the right of war against the parent; and because the parent has no means of support for her offspring except from the master's property, since she has nothing of her own. Since, therefore, the master provides maintenance for such an offspring long before he can be useful by his services, and since his subsequent services do not usually much exceed the cost of maintaining him at the time, he will not be allowed to leave his servitude against the master's will. It is however clear that since such house-born slaves enter slavery by no fault of their own, there is no excuse for treating them more harshly than the condition of perpetual wage-earners admits.

5

On the impulsive cause of constituting the state

1. There seems to be hardly any amenity or advantage that cannot be secured by the duties and conditions [*status*] we have so far discussed. Nevertheless we must now investigate why men have not been content with those first small associations [*societas*], but have constituted large associations which go by the name of states [*civitas*]. For this is the basis from which we must derive the justification of the duties which go with men's civil state [*status civilis*].

2. It is not enough to say here that man is drawn to civil society [*societas civilis*] by nature herself, so that he cannot and will not live without it. For man is obviously an animal that loves himself and his own advantage in the highest degree. It is undoubtedly therefore necessary that in freely aspiring to civil society he has his eye on some advantage coming to himself from it. Again, man was likely to be the most miserable of animals without association [*societas*] with his fellows; yet his natural desires and needs could have been abundantly met by the earliest societies and by duties based on humanity or agreements. We cannot therefore infer directly from man's sociality [*socialitas*] that his nature tends precisely to civil society.

3. This will become clearer if we consider: (1) the human condition which results from the constitution of states; (2) the requirements for a man to be truly said to be a political animal, i.e., a good citizen; and finally, (3) the observed features of human nature which are repugnant tc the character of civil society.

4. (1) In becoming a citizen, a man loses his natural liberty and subjects himself to an authority whose powers include the right of life

and death. At its command he must do much he would otherwise avoid; and he must not do much that he would otherwise powerfully desire to do. Again, in most of his actions he must take into account the good of society, which often seems to conflict with the good of individuals. Yet he has a congenital tendency to want to be subject to no one, to act at his own discretion, and to set his course for his own advantage in everything.

5. (2) By a truly political animal, i.e., a good citizen, we mean one who promptly obeys the orders of those in power; one who strives with all his strength for the public good, and gladly puts his own private good second – one, in fact, who believes nothing to be good for him unless it is also good for the state; one, finally, who is well disposed to his fellow-citizens. But there are few whose natures are spontaneously attuned to this end. Most people are barely restrained by fear of punishment. Many remain bad citizens throughout their lives and not political animals.

6. (3) No animal is fiercer than man, none more savage and prone to more vices disruptive of the peace of society. For besides the desires for food and sex to which the beasts also are subject, man is driven by many vices unknown to them, such as, an insatiable craving for more than he needs, ambition (the most terrible of evils), too-lively remembrance of wrongs, and a burning desire for revenge which constantly grows in force over time; the infinite variety of his inclinations and appetites, and stubbornness in pressing his own causes. And man has such a furious pleasure in savaging his own kind that the greatest part of the evils to which the human condition is subject derives from man himself.

7. Therefore the true and principal cause why heads of households abandoned their natural liberty and had recourse to the constitution of states was to build protection around themselves against the evils that threaten man from man. For just as, after God, man may do more good for his fellow-man than anything else, so he may do most harm. And they judge rightly of the evil of men, and the remedy of that evil, who formulated the saying: 'Without courts of law, men would devour each other.'

But after men had been brought into order by means of states, and so could be safe from injuries from each other, the natural consequence followed of a richer enjoyment of the benefits which tend to come to man from his fellows; for example, the advantage that they are steeped from their earliest years in more suitable habits of behaviour and discover and develop the various skills by which human life has been improved and enriched.

8. The cause of the constitution of states will become still clearer if we reflect that no other means would have been adequate to restrain the evil in man.

Admittedly, natural law teaches that men should refrain from all infliction of injuries. But respect for that law cannot guarantee a life in natural liberty with fair security. There may indeed be men of such good character that they would not want to wrong others even with a guarantee of impunity; others too who would somehow repress their desires through fear of consequent evil. However, there are also a great many men to whom laws mean nothing in the face of an expectation of profit, and who have confidence in their own strength or cunning to repel or elude their victims' vengeance. Everyone who loves his own security seeks to take precautions against such men, and the most appropriate way of taking precautions is by means of states. It is not enough that some persons should have given each other a pledge of mutual assistance; unless there is something which unites their judgements and firmly binds their wills to keep their pledge, it is vain for them to expect sure help from each other.

9. Finally, though natural law gives adequate warning that those who wrong others will not go unpunished, yet neither the fear of God nor the sting of conscience are found to have sufficient force to restrain the evil that is in men. For there are many who, by fault of their upbringing and manner of life, are inattentive to the force of reason. They pay attention only to the present with little care for the future; and are only moved by what is before their eyes.

Divine vengeance tends to proceed at a slow pace; and this gives opportunity to the wicked among mankind to ascribe the sufferings of the impious to other causes, especially as they often see them abundantly provided with those things by which the vulgar measure happiness. There is also the fact that the stings of conscience which precede a crime do not seem to be as strong as those which follow it, when what has been done no longer can be undone. Truly the effective remedy for suppressing evil desires, the remedy perfectly fitted to the nature of man, is found in states.

6

On the internal structure of states

1. We have next to inquire into the means by which states have been instituted and what are their internal bonds of cohesion. In the first place it is clear that the individual finds in other men a more useful and effective defence against the evils that human depravity threatens to inflict on him than in fortifications, weapons or dumb animals; and since a man's power is of limited extent, it was necessary for him to combine with other men to achieve that end.

2. It is equally obvious that a combination of two or three cannot provide that kind of security against other men. For it is easy for enough persons to conspire to overcome these few as would give them full assurance of victory; and their expectation of success and impunity would also give the conspirators the confidence to make the attempt. It is therefore necessary to this end, that there be a union of an overwhelming number of men so that the accession of a few to the enemy would not tip the scales towards victory for the latter.

3. Among these many individuals who come together for this purpose, there has to be a consensus on adopting means likely to achieve it. If they do not agree among themselves, but are distracted in their opinions and tend to different ends, they will achieve nothing, no matter how many they are. Alternatively, there may be a temporary agreement under the impulse of a passion, but they will soon go their separate ways, men's minds and inclinations being as changeable as they are. Though they may promise on the basis of agreement that each will bring his individual strength to the common defence, yet even this method will not provide a guarantee that the group will last. Rather, those who have once consented to peace and mutual help for

the common good must be prohibited from dissenting thereafter, whenever their own private good seems to be in conflict with the public good.

4. There are two principal faults in human nature which prevent a number of independent [*sui juris*] men who are not subordinate to one another from achieving durable cooperation in a common end. One is the diversity of inclinations and judgements in deciding what is most conducive to that end. This is often found in combination with obtuseness in selecting from several options the one which is most advantageous, and a stubbornness in defending tooth and nail whatever option one has taken up. The other fault is indolence, and disinclination to do what is useful, when there is no compulsion to force them to stop procrastinating and to do their duty willy nilly. The first fault is countered by a perpetual union of the wills of all; the second by constituting some power [*potestas*], which shall be directly before their eyes, capable of inflicting suffering on those who oppose the common interest.

5. The only means by which the wills of many may be united is that each submit his will to the will of one man or one assembly, in such a way that from that time on whatever that man or that assembly wills in what concerns the common security be taken as the will of all and everyone.

6. Similarly, such a power as all men may fear can only be constituted among a number of men if each and every one [*omnes & singuli*] obliges himself to use his force as he shall determine to whom all have resigned the direction of their forces.

Only when they have achieved a union of wills and forces is a multitude of men brought to life as a corporate body stronger than any other body, namely a state [*civitas*].

7. Two agreements and one decree are required for a state to form in regular fashion.

First of all, when those many men who are understood to be placed in natural liberty assemble to form a state, they agree one with another individually that they wish to enter into a single and perpetual union and to administer the means of their safety and security by common counsel and leadership; in a word, that they wish to become fellow-citizens. Each and every one must consent to this agreement; anyone who dissents remains outside the future state.

8. After this agreement there must be a decree on the form of

government to be introduced. Until this is determined, no measures of public safety will be able to be effectively instituted.

9. After the decree on the form of government, a second agreement is needed, when the man or men are appointed on whom the government of the infant state is conferred. By this agreement he or they bind himself or themselves to provide for the common security and safety, and the rest bind themselves to obedience to him or them. By this agreement, too, all submit their will to his or their will and at the same time devolve on him or them the use and application of their strength to the common defence. And only when this agreement is duly put into effect does a complete and regular state come into being.

10. A state so constituted is conceived as one person [*persona*], and is separated and distinguished from all particular men by a unique name; and it has its own special rights and property, which no one man, no multitude of men, nor even all men together, may appropriate apart from him who holds the sovereign power or to whom the government of the state has been committed. Hence a state is defined as a composite moral person, whose will blended and combined from the agreement of many is taken as the will of all so that it may employ the forces and capacities of every individual for the common peace and security.

11. The will of the state as the principle of public actions expresses itself either through one man or through one assembly, according as supremacy has been conferred on the one or the other. When the government of the state is in the hands of one man, the state is understood to will whatever he has decided (assuming that he is sane) in anything within the purpose of a state.

12. But when the government of a state has been conferred on an assembly consisting of several men each of whom retains his own natural will, it is normal to take as the will of the state what the majority of those who compose the assembly have agreed to, unless an express arrangement has been made as to what proportion of the assembly is required to give its consent to represent the will of the whole body. When two conflicting opinions have equal weight, no action will be taken, but the matter will remain as it was. When there are several conflicting opinions, that one will prevail which gets more votes than any other, provided that so many agree in it as can represent the will of the whole body in other cases according to public law.

13. In a state so constituted, the bearer of government is called a monarch, a senate or a free people according to whether it is one man, or an assembly of a few, or an assembly of all. The rest are called subjects or citizens, taking the latter word in its wider sense. However, in a narrower sense, the word 'citizens' is often applied only to certain persons by whose union and consent the state was originally formed, or their successors, i.e., the heads of households.

Further, citizens are either native or naturalized. The former are those who either were party to the birth of the state at the beginning, or are descended from them, and are usually called indigenous. The latter are those who come from abroad into a state when it is already formed, to settle there.

Those who are living in a state only for a time, though they are subject to its government during that time, yet are not held to be citizens, but are called foreigners or residents.

14. This account of the origin of states does not imply that civil authority [*imperium civile*] is not rightly said to be of God. For God wills that all men practise natural law, but with the multiplication of mankind such a horrid life was likely to ensue for men that there would scarcely have been a place left for natural law. It is the institution of states which most favours the practice of natural law. And therefore (since he who commands the end is held also to command the necessary means to that end), God too, is understood to have given prior command to the human race, mediated through the dictates of reason, that when it had multiplied, states should be constituted, which are so to speak brought to life by sovereign power. In the Holy Scriptures too He expressly gives His approval to their order and assures the sanctity of that order by special laws and so demonstrates His particular concern for it.

7
On the functions of the sovereign power[1]

1. The functions of the sovereign power [*summi imperii*] and the means by which its force operates in states may be clearly inferred from the nature and purpose of states.

2. In a state all have subjected their own will to the will of those in power in matters affecting the state's security, so that they are willing to do whatever the rulers wish. For this to be possible, those in power must signify to the citizens their will in such matters. They do this not only by instructions addressed to individuals on particular matters, but also by general rules, so that there may always be certainty as to what is to be done and what is not to be done. This is also the normal means by which it is determined what each must regard as his own and what as another's; what is to be taken as lawful in that state, what as unlawful; what as good, what as bad; what remains of each man's natural liberty, or how each must reconcile the enjoyment of his own rights with the tranquillity of the state; and what each man of his own right may require of another and in what manner. Clear definition of all these matters makes a vital contribution to the dignity and tranquillity of the state.

3. The over-riding purpose of states is that, by mutual cooperation and assistance, men may be safe from the losses and injuries which they may and often do inflict on each other. To obtain this from those with whom we are united in one society, it is not enough that we make agreement with each other not to inflict injuries on each other, nor

---

[1] [*De partibus summi imperii*]. '*Imperium*' is translated as 'power' or 'authority' depending on context.

even that the bare will of a superior be made known to the citizens; fear of punishment is needed, and the capacity to inflict it immediately. To achieve its purpose, the penalty must be nicely judged, so that it clearly costs more to break the law than to observe it; the severity of the penalty must outweigh the pleasure or profit won or expected from wrongdoing. For men cannot help choosing the lesser of two evils. Though it is true that there are many men who are not deterred from wrongdoing by threat of punishment, still this must be taken to be exceptional – and the human condition does not allow us to rule out all exceptions.

4. Controversies often arise about the correct application of laws to particular facts, and many points arise that need to be carefully weighed whenever it is alleged that some particular act was illegal. Hence to maintain peace among citizens, it is a function of the sovereign power to take cognizance of the citizens' disputes and make decisions, to investigate actions of individuals denounced as illegal, and to pronounce and execute the penalty in conformity with the laws.

5. To ensure safety against outsiders of those who have united in one state, it is a function of the sovereign power to assemble, unite and arm, or alternatively to hire as many men as may seem necessary for the common defence, taking account of the uncertain number and strength of the enemy, and again, when expedient, to make peace. Alliances have uses in times of war and in times of peace, both to pool better the resources of different states and by a union of forces to repel or bring to terms a stronger enemy. It is therefore within the authority of the sovereign to enter into alliances of both kinds and oblige his subjects to observe them, and at the same time to direct to the state all the benefits flowing from them.

6. The business of a large state, whether in war or in peace, cannot be carried out by one man without ministers and magistrates. The sovereign will therefore need to appoint men who will on his behalf investigate disputes between citizens, gather intelligence of the intentions of neighbouring states, command the soldiers, collect and distribute the state's resources, and, in a word, look to the state's interest [*utilitas*] in every quarter. The sovereign may and should compel all of these officials to do their duty and require them to report to him.

7. The business of the state in war or peace cannot be carried on without expenses. It is the right of the sovereign power, therefore, to compel the citizens to defray these expenses. This may be done in a

variety of ways. For example, the citizens may set aside for this purpose some part of the goods or produce of the region they inhabit; or individual citizens may contribute from their own property and also provide services when needed; or customs duties may be imposed on imports and exports (the former is more of a burden to citizens, the latter to foreigners); or a modest portion of the price of consumer goods may be deducted.

8. Finally, each man governs his actions by his own opinion, but most men usually judge matters as they have been accustomed, and as they see them commonly judged. Very few can discern what is true and good by their own intelligence. It is therefore appropriate for the state that it universally resound with such doctrines as are consistent with the right purpose and usage of states, and that the citizens' minds be steeped in them from childhood. It is a function of sovereignty, therefore, to appoint public teachers of such doctrines.

9. These functions of sovereignty are naturally so interwoven with each other that each and every one of them should be exclusively under the control of one man. For if any one of them is actually missing, the government will be defective and unfitted to achieve the end of a state. But if they are divided, so that some are exclusively under the control of one man, the rest of another, an irregular form of government must result, liable to disintegration.

8

On the forms of government

1. The different forms of government [*respublica*] arise from the vesting of sovereignty in one man or in one assembly consisting of a few or of all.

2. The forms of a state [*civitas*] are either regular or irregular. The form is regular where sovereignty is so concentrated in one subject that, originating in one will, it pervades all the parts and affairs of the state, undivided and unimpaired. Where this is not found, the form of the state will be irregular.

3. There are three forms of a regular state: (1) where sovereignty is in the hands of one man, which is called monarchy; (2) where sovereignty is in the hands of an assembly which consists of selected citizens only, which is called aristocracy; (3) where sovereignty is in the hands of an assembly consisting of all heads of households, which is called democracy. In the first the power-holder is called the monarch, in the second, the nobility, in the third, the people.

4. Power [*potestas*] is indeed the same in each of these forms. But monarchy has a marked advantage over the other forms, in that deliberation and decision, that is, the actual exercise of authority [*imperium*], does not require stated times and places but may occur at any place or time; consequently a monarch is always in full readiness to perform acts of authority. But for decisions to be made by the nobility or the people, neither of which is one natural person, it is necessary that they convene at a fixed time and place for deliberation and decision on public affairs. This is the only way that the will of the senate and the people can be known, since it results from the consenting voices of the majority.

5. But it is the case with sovereignty, as it is with other rights, that it is

well exercised in one place, badly and imprudently in another. Consequently some states are said to be healthy, others sick and corrupt. But we do not need to invent special forms or kinds of government to cover such diseases. Some of the diseases which afflict states are in human beings, others are in the institutions themselves. Hence some are called personal faults, others institutional faults.

6. Personal faults in monarchy arise if the occupant of the throne is destitute of the arts of ruling, and feels little or no responsibility for the country and lets it be wasted by the ambition or avarice of bad ministers; if he terrorizes his subjects by his cruelty and anger; if he takes delight in imperilling his country even without necessity; if he squanders in luxury or senseless largesse what has been collected to meet the expenses of the country; if he accumulates beyond reason monies extorted from the citizens; if he is insolent, if he is unjust; and any other acts which give him the name of a bad prince.

7. Personal faults in aristocracy arise if dishonest or incompetent men make their way into the senate by bribery and underhand methods to the exclusion of their betters; if the nobility is torn by faction; if they endeavour to treat the common people as slaves, and to embezzle public wealth to increase their private fortunes.

8. Personal faults in democracy arise if incompetents and troublemakers make a habit of upholding their opinions in a rude and violent manner; if outstanding talents which pose no danger to the country are suppressed; if laws are made and unmade lightly and in haste and one day's decision is rejected next day without reason; if low and incompetent persons are put in charge of things.

9. Personal faults occurring in any kind of state arise if those on whom the administration of government falls perform their function negligently or badly; and if the citizens, whose only glory is obedience, resist the bridle of the laws.

10. Institutional faults arise when the laws or usages of the state are not suited to the character of the people or of the territory; or when they induce the citizens to form internal factions or to provoke the justified hatred of their neighbours; or if they render them incapable of performing the functions necessary to the preservation of the country: for example, if by the influence of the laws of the state they are inevitably reduced to unwarlike idleness, or rendered unfit to enjoy peace; or if the fundamental laws are so devised that public business cannot be done without delay and difficulty.

11. Special names are often given to such diseased governments, so

that a faulty monarchy is called a tyranny; a faulty form of government of the few is called an oligarchy; a faulty popular form of state is called ochlocracy. Yet it is often the case that in using these terms people are not so much describing a disease of the form of government as expressing their own favour or disfavour towards the current form of government or its rulers. For often an opponent of a king or of the institution of monarchy tends to call even a legitimate and good prince a tyrant or despot, particularly when he enforces the laws strictly. Also, one who resents his exclusion from the senate, since in his own opinion he is not at all inferior to the others who are senators, calls them, in contempt and envy, an oligarchy [*oligous*], which means a certain few who although in no respect superior to others exercise power over their equals or betters in a spirit of disdain.

Finally, when men of proud spirit, who detest popular equality, see every man in a democracy exercising the right of voting on public questions, they call it ochlocracy, since in any state most of the people are plebeians. By ochlocracy they mean a political institution in which the worthless mob is in control, and no prerogative is left to outstanding men (as they think themselves).

12. An irregular form of government [*respublica irregularis*] is one in which we do not find that unity which is the essence of a state so completely established, not because of a disease or fault in the administration of the country, but because the irregularity of its form has been as it were legitimated by public law or custom. There are infinite ways to deviate from correctness, and so in the case of irregular forms of government one cannot define fixed and definite kinds. One can, however, clearly understand the nature of irregular forms from one or two examples. For instance, irregularity occurs in some countries where senate and people handle public business with ultimate right in both parts in such a way that neither is answerable to the other, or in a kingdom where the power of the leading men has grown so great that they are no longer the king's subjects but rather his unequal allies.

13. We speak of 'a system of states' when two or more complete states are connected by some particular bond in such a way that their combined strength may be regarded as the strength of one state. Systems arise in two principal ways: (1) by having a king in common, and (2) by alliance.

14. (1) A system emerges by means of a king in common, when

several separate states have one and the same king, either by agreement or by reason of marriage, inheritance or conquest, provided that they are not amalgamated into one kingdom, but each is governed by the same king in accordance with its own fundamental laws.

15. (2) The second kind of system results when several neighbouring states are so connected by perpetual alliance that they renounce the intention of exercising some portions of their sovereign power, above all those which concern external defence, except with the consent of all, but apart from this the liberty and independence of the individual states remain intact.

9
On the characteristics of civil authority[1]

1. Every authority [*imperium*] by which a state [*civitas*] in its entirety is ruled, whatever the form of government, has the characteristic of supremacy [*summum*]. That is, its exercise is not dependent on a superior; it acts by its own will and judgement; its actions may not be nullified by anyone on the ground of superiority.
2. Hence it is that authority in this sense is unaccountable [*anhupeunthunos*], i.e. not obliged to account to any man on condition that if it should not render him a satisfactory account it would be liable for that reason to human penalty or punishment from him as from a superior.
3. Conformably with this, the sovereign authority [*summum imperium*] is superior to human and civil laws as such, and thus not directly bound by them. For these laws depend in their origins and duration on the sovereign authority. Hence it cannot be that it is bound by them itself, for if it were, the very same power would be superior to itself. Yet, when the sovereign has enjoined certain things on the citizens by law, whose scope extends to him too, it would be appropriate for him to conform of his own free will; this would also tend to strengthen the authority of the law.
4. Sovereign authority, finally, has also its own particular sanctity. It is therefore morally wrong for the citizens to resist its legitimate commands. But beyond this even its severity must be patiently borne by citizens in exactly the same way as good children must bear the ill temper of their parents. And even when it has threatened them with the most atrocious injuries, individuals will protect themselves by

---

[1] [*imperium civile*].

flight or endure any injury or damage rather than draw their swords against one who remains the father of their country, however harsh he may be.

5. In monarchies and aristocracies particularly, sovereign authority occurs in absolute form [*absolutum imperium*]; elsewhere it occurs in limited form.

Absolute authority is said to be held by a monarch who can wield it according to his own judgement, not by following the rule of fixed, standing statutes, but as the actual condition of affairs seems to require, and who uses his own judgement in protecting the security of his country as its circumstances require.

6. But because the judgement of a single man is liable to error and his will may tend towards evil, especially where he has so much liberty, some peoples have thought it prudent to restrain the exercise of authority within fixed limits. This was done at the conferring of the kingship by binding the king to fixed laws concerning the administration of parts of his authority; and for circumstances of supreme crisis if such should arise (and this cannot be defined in advance), they determined that such matters should be handled only with the prior knowledge and consent of the people or of its deputies met in assembly, so that the king would have less opportunity to stray from his kingdom's security.

7. Finally, some differences occur between kingdoms in the manner of holding the kingship, which, one may observe, is not uniform in all kingdoms. For some kings are said to hold their kingdom as a patrimony; they may therefore at their pleasure divide, alienate or transfer it to whom they will. This is particularly the case with kings who have acquired their kingdom by force of arms, and have made their own people for themselves. But those whom the people have freely invited to be king, though they have the highest right to exercise power, yet they may not divide, alienate or transfer the kingdom at their pleasure. They are obliged to follow the fundamental law or accepted custom of the people in handing on the kingdom to their successors, and for this reason some have likened them in a certain respect to usufructuaries.

10

On the ways of acquiring authority, particularly monarchical

1. Consent of subjects is required to constitute any legitimate government, but it is not always and everywhere elicited in the same way. Sometimes men are compelled by military force to consent to a conqueror's rule; sometimes citizens acquiesce of their own accord in the appointment of their prince.

2. Acquisition of authority by military force, which is usually called conquest [*occupatio*], occurs when a man relying upon a just cause for going to war and having been successful by force of arms and fortune reduces a people to the point that they are compelled thenceforth to submit to his authority. The legitimate title of his power is partly drawn from the fact that if he had wished as victor to take advantage of the strict rights of war, he might simply have taken the lives of the vanquished; and thus, by allowing them to get off with a lesser misfortune, he also earns a reputation for clemency. But it is also drawn from the fact that his enemy in going to war with one whom he had previously wronged, and to whom he has refused reasonable satisfaction, has placed all his fortunes on the gaming tables of Mars; he has thus already given tacit consent to whatever condition the event of war may assign him.

3. A kingdom is acquired by the free consent of a people when an election takes place by which a people (whether in process of formation or already formed) freely designates a specific man as in their opinion capable of holding power. The decision [*decretum*] of the people is signified to him; he accepts; the people promise obedience; power is conferred.

4. An election in a state already formed occurring after the death of

the previous king is usually preceded by an interregnum. During this time the state recedes into an imperfect form, as the citizens are then bound together only by the first contract. But a high degree of stability is provided by the love of their common country and its name, and by the fact that for most of the citizens their fortunes are settled there. These motives constrain good citizens to maintain peace with each other of their own accord and to make every effort to restore perfect government as soon as possible. The inconveniences which are apt to arise from interregna can largely be avoided, if there is a prior arrangement as to the interim centre of government during the throne's vacancy.

5. In some places a new election is held whenever a monarch dies. But in others transfer of the kingship to another is regulated by succession without the intervention of an election. The right of succession is established either by the will of the king or by the will of the people.

6. Kings who hold their kingdom as a patrimony can make arrangements about succession at their pleasure. Their arrangements will be respected like the testaments of private persons, especially when a king has founded and acquired his own kingdom. In such a case he may, if he pleases, divide the kingdom among several children, not excluding daughters. He may go further and institute as his heir an adopted or natural son or someone who has no relationship to him at all.

7. But when a king of this kind has made no specific arrangements about the succession, it is usually assumed: that he certainly did not wish the kingship to expire with himself; that in any case by common human feeling he wished it to go to his children; furthermore, that the monarchical form of government to which he gave approval by his own example should be maintained after his death and that the kingship should remain undivided, since division is associated with the splitting apart both of the kingdom and of the royal family; that among equals in degree the male is preferred to the female, the first-born to those born later; finally, that in the absence of children, the kingship devolves on the nearest blood-relative.

8. But in kingships which were formed in the beginning by the free will of a people, the order of succession depends originally on the will of the same people. Where a people has also conferred on the king, together with his authority, the right of appointing his successor, the

king's appointee is the successor. When this has not been done, the people is understood to have reserved this right to itself. If it has pleased the people to confer the kingship (with hereditary right) on an elected king it has either established an order of succession similar to that by simple heredity, so far as the welfare of the kingdom allows, or it has limited it in some particular way.

9. Where a people has authorized a king simply to hold the crown by hereditary right and has set no special conditions, it has expressed a will that the kingship should devolve in the same order as a private inheritance, though with some modification. For the safety of states requires that royal succession should differ from private inheritance in some such points as the following: (1) that the kingdom not be divided; (2) that succession be confined to descendants of the first king; (3) that no illegitimate or adopted children succeed, only those born according to the laws of the country; (4) that of males and females of equal rank, males be preferred to females, even when the females are senior by age; (5) that a successor acknowledge that his crown is a gift from the people, not from his predecessor.

10. Lineal succession was introduced among many peoples, because insoluble controversies could easily arise as to which member of the royal house was most closely related to the deceased, when there was a long distance from the founder of the family. Lineal succession consists of establishing what one might call a perpendicular line of descent for each member from the founder of the reigning family, and calling persons to the throne in the order of precedence of their lines. It also requires that there be no crossing from one line to another so long as anyone survives from the first line, even if perhaps there is someone in another line who is more closely akin to the late king.

11. The most usual kinds of lineal succession are cognate and agnate. In cognate succession females are not excluded, but are placed after males in the same line; and thus recourse is had to them if there is an absence of males of superior or equal degree. Agnate succession, on the other hand, excludes females and even their male children in perpetuity.

12. Whenever a controversy arises about succession in a patrimonial kingdom, it is best to refer it to arbitrators from the royal family. If succession is determined by the will of the people, the uncertainty will be removed by a declaration of the people.

I I

On the duty of sovereigns

1. A clear account of the precepts that govern the office of the sovereign may be drawn from the nature and end of states and from consideration of the functions of sovereignty.

2. The prime requirement is that those in power take pains to learn all that is relevant to a full knowledge of their office; no one can perform with credit what he has not properly learned. Hence the prince must forgo pursuits that have no bearing on his office. Pleasures, amusements and idle pastimes must be cut back, so far as they interfere with this purpose. He should admit to familiarity with himself judicious men skilled in practical affairs; he should ban from his court flatterers and triflers and those who have learned nothing but useless nonsense.

To know how to make a correct application of the general principles of prudent rule, the prince must have the most profound knowledge possible of the conditions of his own position and the character of the people subject to him. He must also particularly cultivate the virtues whose practice is most conspicuous in such large-scale administration and adapt his manners to the dignity of his great eminence.

3. This is the general rule for sovereigns: the safety of the people is the supreme law. For authority has been given them to achieve the end for which states were instituted. Princes must believe that nothing is good for them privately which is not good for the state.

4. The internal peace of the state requires that the wills of the citizens be governed and directed as the safety of the state requires. It is therefore a duty of sovereigns not only to lay down laws appropriate

to that purpose, but also to lend authority to public discipline, so that the citizens conform to the precepts of the laws not so much through fear of punishment as by habituation. It also contributes to this end to ensure that the pure and sincere Christian doctrine flourishes in the state, and that the public schools teach dogmas consistent with the purpose of states.

5. It also contributes to internal peace to have the laws written out plain and clear in the matters that arise most often between citizens. However, the civil laws should regulate only as much as is necessary for the good of state and citizens. For men more often deliberate about what they should or should not do on the basis of natural reason than by knowledge of the law. Hence when there are more laws than they can easily keep in memory, and things are forbidden by law which reason does not by itself forbid, it is inevitable that men should fall foul of the laws even without any wrong intention. Thus those in power may cause the citizens unnecessary inconvenience, and this is contrary to the purpose of states.

6. It is pointless to make laws if sovereigns allow them to be broken with impunity. They therefore have a duty to see that the laws are put into effect and to ensure that each man may obtain his right without lengthy delays, legal evasions and harassment. They must also impose penalties proportionate to the offence in each case and to the intention and malice of the offender. They must not grant pardons without good cause; it is unfair and very exasperating to the citizens not to give similar treatment, other things being equal, to similar offences.

7. Just as penalties should not be imposed except in the public interest, so the public interest should govern the extent of the penalties. In this way the citizens' sufferings will not outweigh the state's gain. Besides, if penalties are to achieve their purpose, they should obviously be designed to ensure that the suffering they inflict outweighs any profit or pleasure that may result from the illegal act.

8. Men have united in states to obtain security against wrongs by others. It is therefore a duty of sovereigns to be severe in preventing men from wronging each other precisely because continual living together offers more frequent opportunity to do harm. Distinctions of rank and dignity ought not to have sufficient influence to allow the more powerful to trample at will on the humbler class. It is also contrary to the purpose of government that citizens should avenge with private violence what they think are wrongs done to them.

9. One prince is unable to deal directly with all the business of a large state. He must inevitably, therefore, call in ministers to share his responsibilities. Nevertheless, as they all derive their power from the sovereign, the responsibility for both their good and their bad actions rests ultimately with him. Again, whether business is handled well or ill depends on the quality of the ministers. For both these reasons, sovereigns have an obligation to employ honest and competent men for the state's offices, and to inquire from time to time into their actions, and to reward or punish them according to their handling of affairs. Thus the rest of the people will understand that public affairs are to be treated with no less sincerity and diligence than their own private affairs. Similarly, wicked men are attracted to commit crimes by the hope of avoiding punishment, and their hope is liveliest when judges are open to corruption. Consequently, it is the duty of sovereigns to impose severe punishment on such judges; they encourage crime which destroys the citizens' security. Finally, although the handling of business should be left to ministers, sovereigns should never refuse to lend a patient ear to the complaints and petitions of the citizens.

10. The only ground on which citizens must bear taxes and other burdens is so far as these are necessary to meet the state's expenses in times of war and peace. It is therefore the duty of sovereigns in this matter not to extract more than the necessities or major interests of the country require; and to keep the burdens as light as possible, so that the citizens suffer as little as possible. Then they must ensure that taxes are assessed fairly and proportionately, and that immunities are not granted to some part of the citizens to defraud and exploit the rest. What is collected must be spent on the state's requirements, not squandered in extravagance, largesse, unnecessary ostentation or frivolity. Finally, one must ensure that expenditures correspond with revenues; when revenues fall short, the solution must be found in economy and retrenchment of unnecessary expenses.

11. Sovereigns are not obliged to maintain their subjects, though, exceptionally, charity requires them to take particular care of those who cannot support themselves because of some undeserved misfortune. Nevertheless, sovereigns must not merely collect from the citizens' property the funds necessary for the preservation of the state. For the strength of the state consists also in the virtue and wealth of the citizens, and therefore the sovereign must take whatever measures

he can to ensure the growth of the citizens' personal prosperity. A step in this direction is to develop in the citizens the attitude that they should draw a rich harvest from the land and its waters; that they should apply their industry to their country's natural resources, not purchasing from others the labour which they can well perform themselves; and to achieve this, sovereigns must encourage technical skills. It is also supremely important to promote trade and encourage navigation in the coastal districts. Idleness has to be banished; and the citizens recalled to habits of economy by sumptuary laws which prohibit excessive expenditures, especially those by which the citizens' wealth is transferred abroad. Here the example set by sovereigns is more effective than any law.

12. The internal health and stability of states results from the union of the citizens, and the more perfect it is, the more effectively the force of government will pervade the whole body of the state. It is therefore the sovereign's task to ensure that factions do not arise; to prevent citizens from forming associations by private agreements; to ensure that neither all nor some have a greater dependence on any other person whether within or without the state, under whatever guise, sacred or profane, than on their own prince, and that they believe they have more protection for themselves from him than from anyone else.

13. Finally, the relation of states to each other is a somewhat precarious peace. It is therefore a duty of sovereigns to take measures to develop military virtue and skill with weapons in the citizens, and to make ready in good time all that is needed for repelling force: fortified places, weapons, soldiers and – the sinews of action – money. But one should not take the initiative in aggression even with a just cause for war, unless a perfectly safe opportunity occurs and the country's condition can easily bear it. To the same end one must obtain accurate intelligence of the plans and projects of one's neighbours, and use prudence in contracting friendships and alliances.

12

On civil laws in particular

1. It remains to discern the specific functions of sovereign power and their noteworthy features. Most important here are the civil laws, which are the decrees of the sovereign civil authority [*summi imperantis civilis*], which enjoin upon the citizens what they should do or not do in civil life.

2. There are two particular senses in which the word 'civil' is applied to law: with respect to authority and with respect to origin. In the former sense, all laws are called civil which are the bases for the giving of justice in the civil courts, whatever their origin. In the latter sense, those laws are called civil which proceed from the will of the sovereign and deal with matters which are undefined by natural and divine law but deeply affect the private interests of individual citizens.

3. Though nothing should be regulated by the authority of the civil laws unless it has a bearing on the public interest, it is of the highest importance for the dignity and peace of civil life that citizens should properly observe the natural law; and therefore it is a duty of sovereigns to lend it the force and effectiveness of civil law. For there is so much wickedness in the greater part of mankind that neither the obvious benefits of natural law nor fear of divine power is adequate to check it. The sovereign, therefore, may ensure preservation of the moral integrity of civil life by lending to natural laws the force of the civil laws.

4. The force of the civil laws consists in the addition of a penal sanction to precepts to do or not to do, or in defining the penalty in the courts that awaits one who has done what he ought not or not done what he ought. Violations of natural law which have no penal

sanctions attached are beyond the reach of human justice, though the divine tribunal still stands ready to punish.

5. Since civil life is too fragile to allow each man to exact what he believes to be his due by violent self-help, civil laws come to the aid of natural law in providing actions for the obligations of natural law. Such actions enable a man to exact his due in civil courts with the help of a magistrate. What is not backed by this force of the civil laws cannot be wrested from one who refuses to give it, but depends wholly on the delicacy of the delinquent's conscience.

It is normal that civil laws provide actions chiefly for obligations arising from explicit contracts between parties. They have usually refused actions for other obligations based on some indefinite duty of natural law. The intention here is that good men should have scope to exercise their virtue, and to win public commendation for being seen to have acted well without compulsion. Often too matters have seemed too trivial to justify troubling the judge with them.

6. Many of the precepts of natural law are indefinite, and their application is left to each man's own discretion. In its concern for the dignity and peace of the community the civil law normally prescribes time, manner, place and persons for actions of this kind, defines other relevant circumstances and sometimes provides rewards to induce men to obey. The civil law has also the function of clarifying whatever is obscure in natural law; citizens are obliged to accept this clarification, though their private opinions may be quite different.

7. Again, in a state most actions are left by natural law to the judgement and discretion of the individual, but they need to be managed in a uniform way in the interest of public peace and dignity. Hence civil laws normally prescribe a fixed form for actions and transactions of that kind, for example wills, contracts and many others. For the same reason civil laws have usually put limits on the exercise of rights admissible by nature.

8. Citizens ought to obey the civil laws, so far as they are not openly repugnant to divine law, not as if by fear of punishment alone, but by an internal obligation which is established by natural law itself, since its precepts include the behest to obey legitimate rulers.

9. Finally, citizens must obey particular commands of rulers no less than the common laws. But here a question arises: does what the sovereign orders the citizen to do become the citizen's own action? Or does the sovereign rather merely assign to him the execution of an act

which is to be regarded as the sovereign's own? For in the latter case the citizen, acting under compulsion from the ruler, can do, without wrong on his part, acts whose commission involves the ruler in wrongdoing. But a citizen is never justified in doing anything contrary to natural and divine law in his own name. Hence it is that, if a citizen bears arms on the orders of the sovereign even in an unjust war, he does not do wrong. But if on the sovereign's orders he condemns the innocent, bears false witness or brings mischievous accusation against someone, he does undoubtedly do wrong. For a citizen bears arms in the public name; but it is in his own name that he acts as judge, witness and accuser.

13
On the right of life and death

1. The sovereign civil authority has a twofold right over the citizens' lives: a direct right in the suppression of crime, and an indirect right in the defence of the state.

2. Force on the part of an external enemy has often to be met by force; or we may need to use violence in claiming our right. In either case the sovereign authority may compel the citizens to perform this kind of service, where it is not a question of deliberately sending them to death but only of exposing them to the danger of death. The sovereign authority has the duty to give them training and preparation to conduct themselves with vigour and skill in such dangers. No citizen through fear of this danger may render himself unfit for military service. Once inducted, he will in no circumstances desert his post through fear but will fight rather to the last breath, unless he believes it to be the will of his commander that he should save his life rather than hold his position, or that the position is less important to the state than the lives of the citizens involved.

3. Executing its right directly the sovereign power may take away citizens' lives for atrocious crimes and as a punishment (though punishment also falls upon a man's other possessions). At this point a few general explanatory remarks on the nature of punishment are necessary.

4. A punishment is an evil one suffers, inflicted in return for an evil one has done; in other words, some painful evil imposed by authority as a means of coercion in view of a past offence.

(1) For although punishment often takes the form of action, yet

these actions are designed to be laborious and painful to the doer and so to inflict on him a kind of suffering.

(2) Punishment is to be inflicted on men against their will. Otherwise it would not achieve its goal, which is to deter men from wrongdoing by its harshness. Nothing a man gladly accepts has this effect.

(3) Evils inflicted in war or in self-defence in fighting are not punishments, because they are not by authority.

(4) Nor is what one suffers when wronged a punishment, because it is not inflicted in view of a past offence.

5. It is characteristic of natural liberty that a man in that state has no superior except God and is therefore liable only to divine punishment. By contrast, with the introduction of government among men, the security of societies requires that rulers too have the capacity to suppress the wickedness of their subjects upon the commission of an offence, so that most men may live securely with one another.

6. Although there is nothing obviously inequitable in an evildoer suffering evil, still when human beings inflict punishments they have to consider not only what evil was done, but also what good may come from its punishment. For example one should never inflict punishments to gratify the victim's delight in the pain and punishment of his attacker. For this delight is clearly inhumane and repugnant to sociality.

7. The real aim of punishment by human beings is the prevention of attacks and injuries. This aim is achieved if the criminal changes for the better, or others by his example no longer wish henceforth to do wrong; or if the criminal is restrained so that he can do no more harm. This can be expressed as follows: the purpose of punishment is either the good of the criminal, or the interest of the person for whom it would have been better if the crime had not been committed and who has thus been injured by the crime, or everyone's interest without distinction.

8. The first purpose then of punishment is the good of the offender; his character is reformed by the pain of the punishment itself, which also extinguishes his desire to do wrong. Even in states, most commonly, this kind of punishment is left to heads of households to exercise on members of their households. Given its purpose it may not go to the length of inflicting death, since a dead man cannot be reformed.

9. Second, punishment also seeks the interest of the victim, which is that he should not suffer the same thing again either from the same man or from others. The former object is attained either by getting rid of the offender altogether, or by taking away his capacity to do harm while sparing his life, or if as a result of punishment he learns not to offend. The latter object is attained by public and open punishment designed to strike terror into others.

10. Finally, punishment aims at the good of all, in that it is concerned with preventing someone who has harmed one man from subsequently harming another, or with deterring others from similar acts by fear of his example. This object is attained in the same way as the former.

11. If we reflect on the purposes of punishment and the condition of the human race, it becomes clear that not all offences are fit to be punished by human justice. The following are exempt from human punishment:

(1) Purely internal acts, i.e. delicious thoughts of sin, greed, desire and intention without action, even if subsequent confession reveals them to others. For no harm is done to anyone by such an internal impulse; and it is in no one's interest that anyone be punished for it.

12. (2) It would also be excessively rigorous to subject petty lapses to human penalties. In the condition of nature in which we live no one can avoid such lapses however scrupulous he may be.

13. (3) Further, human laws turn a blind eye to many acts, for the peace of civil society or for other reasons: for example, if some action would be more splendid if punishment was not seen to be a factor in its undertaking; or when it is not worth troubling the judges over a minor incident; or if a case is too obscure for a clear verdict; or if an abuse is too deeply ingrained to be removed without turning the country upside down.

14. (4) Finally, we must also exempt from human punishment those faults of character which arise from man's common corruption. They occur so commonly that you would have no one left to rule, if you chose to visit them with severe penalties, so long as they have not erupted into serious crimes, for

example, ambition, avarice, inhumanity, ingratitude, hypo-
crisy, envy, arrogance, anger, animosity, and so on.

15. However, even in the case of offences deserving punishment, it is
not always necessary to impose penalties. In fact, it happens from time
to time that an offender may rightly be granted a pardon for his crime.
This should not however be done without very good reasons, among
which are the following: if the purposes of punishment in a given case
seem not to be appropriate; or if a pardon would produce more good
than a penalty; or if the purposes of punishment can be more readily
achieved some other way. Likewise if the transgressor adduces services to his country on his part or on the part of his kin which deserve
special reward; or if he is recommended by any other outstanding
attribute, as some rare skill; or if there is hope that he will purge his
fault by distinguished achievements; especially where some ignorance
is involved, even if not altogether inculpable; or if the particular
reason for the law is inapplicable to the act in question. Often, too,
pardon must be granted because there are so many offenders that
punishing them all would exhaust the state.

16. The gravity of offences is determined as follows: from the object
on which the offence was committed, its dignity and value; similarly,
from its effect, whether it causes much or little damage to the country;
and from the wickedness of the motive, which may be assessed from
various signs: for example, if the offender might easily have resisted
the causes impelling him to do wrong; or if in addition to the usual
deterrents, there was some particular reason that should have
restrained him from wrongdoing; or when there are aggravating
circumstances; or if his temperament fitted him to resist temptations
to do wrong. Other usual considerations are whether a man took the
lead or was seduced by the example of others, or whether he offended
repeatedly and after several wasted warnings.

17. The precise kind and amount of punishment to be inflicted in
individual cases are for the supreme civil authority to determine,
whose only object here must be the good of the country. Hence it may
and does happen that two unequal crimes may incur the same penalty.
For the equality which judges are instructed to observe in the matter
of defendants is to be understood of defendants who have committed
crimes of the same kind, insofar as the offence which is condemned in
one should not be condoned in the other without very good reason.

And although men should, so far as possible, be rather gentle towards their fellow-men, nevertheless from time to time the safety of the state and the security of the citizens require that penalties be made more severe: for example, if strong medicine is needed against a growth in crime, or where some offence is particularly dangerous to the state. What must always be kept in view in estimating penalties is that they should be adequate to curb the passion by which men are driven to the crime for which the penalty provides. One should not exact heavier penalties than are set by law, unless particularly atrocious circumstances aggravate the offence.

18. However, the same penalty does not affect all men equally and so does not have the same effect in curbing the desire to do wrong. Hence in the general assessment of penalties and in their application to individuals you must take account of the person of the actual offender and of the qualities in him which may increase or diminish his reaction to the penalty, for example, age, sex, status, wealth, strength, and so on.

19. Just as (in human justice) no one can be punished for another man's crime, so if a crime has been committed by a corporation, anyone who did not consent to it will not be guilty of it. Hence if a man did not consent, he can only be made to forfeit what he received in the name of and for the benefit of the corporation, though the innocent too usually do suffer loss as a result of the punishment of a corporation. The offences of public bodies expire when none of those by whose consent and co-operation the crime was committed remain alive.

20. Yet it often happens that one man's offence causes another's loss or the disappointment of some expected good. For example, if parents' wealth is confiscated for an offence, the innocent children are also reduced to poverty. And if a defendant skips bail, the bonds-man is compelled to pay a fine, not for an offence, but because it was precisely in case such a thing happened that he undertook the obligation.

14

On reputation

1. Reputation in general is the value of persons in common life [*vita communis*] by which they may be measured against others or compared with them and either preferred or put after them.

2. Reputation is either simple or intensive. Both are viewed with reference on the one hand to men living in natural liberty and on the other hand to men in the civil state.

3. Simple reputation among those who live in natural liberty consists primarily in each man's making himself and being taken to be such a man as may be dealt with as a good man and who is fit to live with others by the prescript of natural law.

4. Reputation of this kind is held to be intact, so long as one does not knowingly, willingly and with evil intent violate the law of nature with respect to others by a malicious or outrageous act. Hence everyone is taken to be a good man, until the contrary is proved.

5. Reputation of this kind is diminished by malicious commission of outrageous crimes contrary to the law of nature, the effect of which is that one needs to show more caution in dealing with such a man. However, this stain may be purged by making voluntary reparation for the loss caused and by giving evidence of sincere repentance.

6. Similarly, reputation is utterly destroyed by a manner and way of life which aims directly at indiscriminate harm to others and at profiting by open wrongdoing. Men of this nature (so long as they show no signs of repentance) may be treated as public enemies by all who are in any way affected by their wickedness. They may however repair their reputation by abjuring their vicious manner of life and entering

on an honourable course, after making restitution for loss or obtaining forgiveness.

7. Simple reputation among those who live in states is not to have been declared by the law and custom of the state a vicious member of the same, and to be regarded as a person of some standing.

8. Want of simple reputation may be a result merely of status or it may be a result of crime.

Want of simple reputation as a result of status applies to two cases: when the status in question has naturally in itself nothing disgraceful or else when it is associated with vice or at least with a perception of vice. The former occurs in some states, where there are slaves with no standing. The latter is the case with pimps and prostitutes and such like: they do indeed enjoy public protection so long as they are publicly tolerated, but they should be excluded from the company of honest men. The same is the case with those whose occupations, though not vicious in nature, are sordid or mean.

9. Total loss of simple reputation may also be the result of crime, when a man is marked with infamy by the civil laws; he may also be executed, in which case his memory is damned; or exiled from the state; or permitted to remain in the state as an infamous and unsavoury character.

10. It is clear that simple reputation or natural honesty cannot be taken from a man by the arbitrary decision of sovereigns, since it cannot be thought to be in the state's interest in any way that this power should be conferred upon them. Likewise, it does not seem possible to incur true infamy so long as one is executing the state's law in the simple capacity of a minister.

11. Intensive reputation is that by which some persons, though otherwise equal to others in terms of simple reputation, are given preference over them, insofar as there are qualities in one more than in the other which move men's minds to honour them. And indeed honour properly so called is the indication of our judgement of another's superiority.

12. This intensive reputation may be considered in respect either to those who live in natural liberty or to citizens of the same state. We must also examine the grounds of such reputation both where they simply make it appropriate to expect honour from others, and where they give rise to a right strictly so called to require honour from others as one's due.

13. The grounds of intensive reputation in general are considered to be everything that has a notable degree of perfection and superiority, or is judged to give evidence of such, provided their effect is congruous with the purpose of natural law or of states: for instance, intelligence and a capacity to master various skills and disciplines, a keen judgement in managing affairs, a firm temper unshaken by external events and superior to temptation and fear, eloquence, physical beauty and dexterity, the good things of fortune and, above all, outstanding achievements.

14. All these qualities, however, yield only an imperfect right or aptitude to receive honour and respect from others. Hence to refuse such honour to others even when they have deserved it is not wrong but only disreputable as a mark of inhumanity and what one might call 'incivility'. But a perfect right to receive honour or the outward signs of honour from another arises either from the authority which one has over him, or from an agreement one has made with him, or else from a law made or sanctioned by their common master.

15. Between princes and between independent peoples the factors specially cited for pre-eminence and precedence are: antiquity of kingdom and dynasty; extent and wealth of subject territories and power; the nature of the authority by which one holds power in the kingdom and the splendour of the title. But these factors in themselves do not create a perfect right to precedence as against other kings or peoples, unless it has been acquired by agreement or concession on their part.

16. Among citizens it is the prerogative of the sovereign to assign degrees of dignity, but in this matter he is right to have regard for each man's excellence and his capacity to do services for his country. Whatever degree of dignity the sovereign has assigned to a citizen, he must protect it against the man's fellow-citizens; and he should acknowledge it equally himself.

15

On the power of sovereign authority over property within the state

1. When property has come to citizens from sovereigns, the right by which they hold it depends on the discretion of the sovereign. By contrast, property of which citizens have obtained full ownership by their own industry or in any other way is subject to three principal rights which, by the nature of states and as necessary to their purpose, belong to sovereigns.

2. The first right is that sovereigns may make laws obliging the citizens to accommodate their use of their property to the interest of the state; or defining the extent and nature of possessions, and the method of transferring property to others, and other matters of this kind.

3. The second right is that the sovereign may collect a fraction of the citizens' property as tribute or tax. For since their lives and fortunes are to be defended by the state, it is appropriate that they contribute to meeting the expenses necessary to this end. It is totally unscrupulous to attempt to enjoy the protection and convenience the state affords while refusing to contribute either service or property to its preservation. And yet prudent rulers would be wise to take into consideration the resentment felt by ordinary people, and to make an effort to give as little offence as possible in collecting taxes, observing fairness above all and imposing taxes that are moderate and flexible rather than massive and uniform.

4. The third right is eminent domain, which means that in a national emergency sovereigns may seize and apply to public use the property of any subject which the crisis particularly requires, even if the property seized far exceeds the amount which had been fixed as his normal

obligatory contribution to his country's expenses. For this reason, however, as much of the excess as possible should be refunded to him from the public treasury or by a levy on the rest of the citizens.
5. Besides these three rights, there is in many states a distinct public property, which usually goes under the name of the country's or the kingdom's patrimony. This is again divided in various places into the patrimony of the prince and that of the country, or into the privy purse and the treasury. The former is intended for the maintenance of the king and his family, the latter for the public purposes of the kingdom. The king has a usufruct of the former and may dispose of the proceeds from it as he pleases. In the case of the latter, however, he is in the position of an administrator, and should apply this fund to the uses for which it is intended. He can alienate neither without the consent of the people.
6. There is even less of a case for a king who does not hold his kingdom as a patrimony to alienate the whole kingdom or any part of it without the consent of the people; and in this latter case, without the particular consent of the part to be alienated. Conversely, no member territory of a state may break away from it without the state's consent, unless reduced by force of external enemies to such a condition that it can not survive in any other way.

16

On war and peace

1. It is most agreeable to natural law that men should live in peace with each other by doing of their own accord what their duty requires; indeed peace itself is a state peculiar to man, insofar as he is distinct from the beasts. Nevertheless, for man too war is sometimes permitted, and occasionally necessary, namely when by the ill will of another we cannot preserve our property or obtain our right without the use of force. In this situation, however, good sense and humanity counsel us not to resort to arms when more evil than good is likely to overtake us and ours by the prosecution of our wrongs.

2. The just causes of engaging in war come down to the preservation and protection of our lives and property against unjust attack, or the collection of what is due to us from others but has been denied, or the procurement of reparations for wrong inflicted and of assurance for the future. Wars waged for the first of these causes are said to be defensive, for the other causes, offensive.

3. One should not have immediate recourse to arms as soon as one thinks oneself wronged, particularly so long as there remains some doubt about right or fact. One should explore the possibility of amicable settlement of the matter by various means, for example by initiating dialogue between the parties, by appealing to an arbitrator, or by submitting the question to lot. The claimant particularly is obliged to try this method, since there is in any case a predisposition to favour possession with some title.

4. Unjust causes of war are either openly such or have some plausible pretext, however weak. Open causes come down to two main types: avarice and ambition, namely lust for wealth and lust for power.

Those covered by pretexts are various: they include fear of the wealth and power of a neighbour, unjustified aggrandizement, desire for better territory, refusal of something which is simply and straightforwardly owed, stupidity on the part of a possessor, a desire to extinguish another's legitimately acquired right which the aggressor finds rather inconvenient, and others of this kind.

5. The most proper forms of action in war are force and terror. But one has equal right to use fraud and deceit against an enemy, provided one does not violate one's pledged faith. Hence one may deceive an enemy by false statements or fictitious stories, but never by promises or agreements.

6. As for force used in war against an enemy and his property, one must distinguish between what an enemy may suffer without wrong and what we ourselves may inflict without loss of humanity. When a man has declared himself my enemy, he has by that fact made known his intention to inflict the last degree of suffering on me, and by that same fact he grants me, so far as he can, an unlimited right against himself. Humanity however requires that so far as the momentum of warfare permits, we should inflict no more suffering on an enemy than defence or vindication of our right and its future assurance requires.

7. War is normally divided into two forms: declared and undeclared. There are two necessary conditions of a declared war: first that it be waged by the authority of the sovereigns on both sides, and secondly that it be preceded by a declaration. Undeclared war is either war waged without formal declaration or war against private citizens. Civil wars also are in this category.

8. The right of initiating war in a state lies with the sovereign. It is beyond the capacity of an official to exercise that right without the authority delegated to him by the sovereign to do so, even in a situation in which he infers that the sovereign, if consulted, would decide upon immediate war. However, all who have charge of a province or fortified place with military forces under their command are understood to be obliged by the nature of their office to repel an invading enemy from the area entrusted to them by whatever means they can. But they should not without grave cause move the war on to the enemy's territory.

9. Whereas one who lives in natural liberty may be pursued in war only for wrongs he has committed himself, in civil society the ruler of

a state or the state as a whole is often attacked, even though he or it was not the source of the wrong. But for this to be justified, it is essential that the wrong pass in some way to the ruler. And in fact rulers of states do share in wrongs committed by their long-settled citizens or by those who have recently taken refuge with them, if the rulers allowed the commission of the wrongs or provide refuge. For such allowance to be culpable, there must be a knowledge of the crime and ability to prevent it. Rulers are presumed to be aware of the open and habitual actions of their citizens, and there is always a presumption of their ability to prevent them, unless there is obvious evidence of its absence. However, the right to make war upon a ruler who accepts and protects a delinquent, who is seeking refuge with him solely to escape punishment, arises more from particular agreements between neighbours and allies than from any common obligation. This is not the case, however, if the refugee while with us is planning hostilities against the state he has left.

10. It is also accepted among nations that the goods of private citizens may be held for a debt which is properly the state's or for something which the state confiscated without observing the requirements of justice, so that foreigners to whom the debt is due may impound any goods of citizens from the debtor state which they find on their own territories. In such cases, however, the citizens whose goods have been taken in this way should obtain restitution from the actual debtors. Such exactions are known as reprisals and are frequently preludes to war.

11. One may wage war on another's behalf as well as for oneself. This is justified where the party for whom one is going to war has a just cause, and where the party coming to aid has a reasonable ground for conducting hostilities on his behalf against the third party.

The first among those for whom we not only may but should take up arms are our subjects both as a whole and as individuals, provided that the state would not evidently be involved in greater suffering as a result. Then come allies who have a treaty which includes this provision. However, they yield precedence to our own citizens, if the latter need our help at the same moment; and it is assumed that they have a just cause of war and that they are showing some prudence in undertaking it. Next in order are friends, even if no such specific promise has been given them. And finally, where no other ground exists, kinship alone may suffice for us to go to the defence of an oppressed party who makes a plea for assistance, so far as we conveniently may.

12. The extent of licence in war is such that, however far one may have gone beyond the bounds of humanity in slaughter or in wasting and plundering property, the opinion of nations does not hold one in infamy nor as deserving of being shunned by honest men. However, the more civilized nations condemn certain ways of inflicting harm on an enemy: for instance, the use of poison or bribing the citizens or soldiers of other rulers to assassinate them.

13. Movable property is considered to be captured from the moment that it is beyond enemy pursuit, immovable property when we hold it so effectively as to have the ability to keep the enemy off it. However, the condition of the absolute extinction of the former owner's right of recovery is his renunciation by subsequent agreement of all claim to it. Otherwise what is ours by force may be taken back by force.

As soldiers fight by the authority of the state, so what they take from the enemy is acquired for the state, not for themselves. However, it is a universal practice that movable property, especially if of no great value, is tacitly left to the soldiers who took it, either as a reward, or sometimes in lieu of pay, or to give incentive to men to put their lives on the line without compulsion.

When captured property is taken back from an enemy, immovable property returns to its former owners. So too should movable property, but among most peoples it is left to the soldiers as booty.

14. Rule over conquered peoples as over individuals is also won by war. For it to be legitimate and binding upon the consciences of subjects, the conquered must swear loyalty to the conquerors and the conquerors give up their state of enmity and hostile intention towards the conquered.

15. Acts of war are suspended by a truce, which is an agreement to refrain from acts of war for a period of time, without ending the state of war or settling the dispute from which the war started. When the period of the truce has expired, there is a return to a state of war without a new declaration, unless peace has been made in the meantime.

16. Truces may be divided into those which are made with the armies remaining in the field and fighting readiness maintained on both sides (the period of such truces is fairly short), and truces in which fighting readiness is disbanded on both sides. The latter may be made

for quite long periods of time and normally are; they have the appearance of complete peace, and sometimes are even termed peace with the specification of a fixed period of time. For otherwise every peace is assumed to be perpetual and to lay permanently to rest the disputes from which the war broke out. The arrangements normally called tacit truces impose no obligation; in such cases the parties remain quiet on both sides at their discretion and may resume acts of war whenever they so please.

17. A war is definitively ended only when peace is ratified by the sovereigns on both sides. Both the parties to the agreement must define its terms and conditions, and have equally the obligation to put them into effect at the agreed time, and to observe them faithfully. To assure this, an oath is normally included and hostages given, and often other parties, particularly those who take part in the peace-making, accept the duty of ensuring compliance by promising aid to the party which is injured by the other contrary to the terms of the peace.

17
On treaties[1]

1. Treaties which are agreements made between independent sovereign rulers have a function both in wartime and in peacetime. They may be divided, on the basis of their content, into those which define the terms of reciprocal performance of some duty already enjoined by natural law, and those which go beyond the duties of natural law, or at least put into specific terms what seems indefinite in natural law.

2. Treaties of the first type are those which form an agreement merely about practising simple humanity or refraining from doing harm. To this category belong also treaties which simply give formal expression to friendly relations without any requirements or which confirm the right of diplomacy and commerce insofar as it is laid down by natural law.

3. Treaties of the second type are either equal or unequal. An equal treaty is the same for both parties. It involves equality in the content of the promises made on each side, either simply or with due regard to differences of strength, and equality in the manner of the promises, so that neither party may be in an inferior position to the other or subject to him.

4. Treaties are unequal when the performances promised by the parties are unequal or when one party is in an inferior position to the other. Unequal promises are made either by the more powerful party to the treaty or by the less powerful. The first is the case if the greater power promises help to the other party without a stipulation in return,

---

[1] Or 'On alliances' [De Foederibus].

or if it makes promises on a larger scale than the other. The second is the case if the weaker party is obliged to give more than it gets back. 5. Some of the obligations of a weaker party to a treaty involve some loss of sovereignty, for example if it is agreed that the weaker ally may not exercise some part of his sovereign power without the consent of the more powerful. Some, however, involve no loss of sovereignty even though they entail some temporary burden, that is, a burden which may be discharged once and for all, for example an obligation by the treaty of peace to pay the other party's troops; an indemnity of war expenses; payment of a fixed sum of money; destruction of walls; giving of hostages; surrender of ships, arms, etc. In fact there are even some permanent burdens which involve no loss of sovereignty, such as a unilateral obligation to have the same friends and enemies as the other party; a prohibition on building fortifications in certain places or on sailing to certain places, etc.; likewise, if one of the allies is required to treat the majesty of the other ally with deference or to show him a certain respect and to acquiesce in his will with due discretion.

6. There is a variety of reasons for making treaties, whether equal or unequal. Among these reasons, those which look to a permanent union between several states give rise to treaties of the closest kind. But the most frequent type of treaty is that whose object is the provision of assistance in a defensive or offensive war or the regulation of commerce.

7. Treaties are also frequently distinguished as real or personal. Personal treaties are made with a king in his own person, and expire on his death. Real treaties are made not so much with the king or rulers of the people as such as with the country and the kingdom, and persist despite the deaths of those who were their authors.

8. Related to treaties are agreements in principle [*sponsiones*]. This term properly refers to agreements made by the minister of a sovereign on matters that concern the sovereign but without his authorization. The sovereign is not bound by them unless he subsequently ratifies them. Consequently if the minister has made an absolutely binding agreement and ratification does not follow, it is his responsibility to make reparation to those who accepted his word and have been deceived by worthless agreements.

18

On the duties of citizens

1. A citizen's duty is either general or special. General duties arise from the common obligation to be subject to the civil authority. Special duties arise from the particular tasks and functions which the sovereign may impose upon individuals.

2. A citizen's general duties are towards either the governors of the state, or the state as a whole, or his fellow-citizens.

3. The citizen owes respect, loyalty and obedience to the governors of his state. This entails that he be content with the actual state of things and not give his mind to revolution, and that he not form too close ties with any other ruler nor show him admiration and respect. In thought and speech he should honour and approve his governors and their actions.

4. The duty of a good citizen to the state as a whole is that its safety and security be his dearest wish; that his life, wealth and fortune be freely offered to preserve it; that he devote all the vigour of his intelligence and industry to extend its glory and increase its prosperity.

5. A citizen's duty towards his fellow-citizens is to live with them in peace and friendship; to be courteous and obliging; not to cause trouble by being stubborn and difficult; not to covet or steal other people's property.

6. Special duties are concerned either with the whole state indifferently or with only a part of it. In all cases the general precept holds: no one should accept or undertake any public duty for which he believes himself unfit.

7. Those who assist the governors of the state with counsel must keep

an eye on all parts of the country; whatever seems good for it they should skilfully and faithfully propose, without fear or favour; the country's welfare must be their aim in all their counsels, not their own wealth or power; they should not encourage by flattery evil inclinations on the part of princes; they must avoid illegal factions and associations; they should not keep to themselves what should be published, nor broadcast what should be kept confidential; they should be impervious to corruption by foreigners; and they should give priority to public business over private business or pleasures.

8. The publicly appointed ministers of religion should show dignity and scrupulousness in the performance of their duties; they must declare true dogmas on the worship of the Deity; they should make themselves conspicuous examples of what they teach the people; and they should not cheapen the worth of their office or weaken the influence of their teaching by their own moral failings.

9. Those who have been given the responsibility of instructing citizens in the various branches of learning should teach nothing false or harmful. Their manner in teaching what is true should bring their students to assent to the truth not so much because they have heard it often as because they have understood the solid grounds for it; they should avoid all dogmas which tend to disturb civil society; they should hold that all human knowledge which is not useful for human and civil life is worthless.

10. There must be easy access to those who are charged with the administration of justice; they must protect the common people from oppression by the powerful; they must give justice equally to the poor and humble and to the powerful and influential; they must not drag out legal cases more than necessary; they must abjure bribes; they must show diligence in hearing cases and put aside any prejudices that would mar the integrity of their judgements; and they should not fear any man in doing what is right.

11. Those who are entrusted with the armed forces should take care to train the soldier in due time and inure him to the rigours of military life; to keep military discipline in good order; not rashly expose their soldiers to be massacred by the enemy; and promptly supply pay and provisions, so far as they can, embezzling nothing. They must also ensure that the troops always support their country and never conspire with them against it.

12. For their part soldiers should be content with their pay; refrain

from pillage and harassment of the population; perform their tasks in protection of their country gladly and with vigour; not rashly court danger nor avoid it through cowardice; show courage against the enemy, not against their comrades; and choose rather to die with honour than to save their lives by running away.

13. Those who are sent abroad on state business need to be cautious and circumspect; shrewd in distinguishing good information from the worthless and the true from the fabricated; utterly discreet in keeping secrets; inflexible for their country's good against all possible corruption.

14. Those who have charge of collecting and spending state revenues should refrain from all unnecessary harshness and not impose any additional charge for their own gain or from spite or annoyance; not embezzle public funds; and pay those who have a claim on the treasury without unnecessary delay.

15. A citizen's special duty lasts as long as he remains in the position which gives rise to the duty; when he leaves, the duty too expires. General duties last as long as a man remains a citizen.

Citizenship ceases if a person leaves his country with its express or tacit consent to settle elsewhere; or if he is sent into exile for crime and is deprived of the right of citizenship; or if he is overcome by an enemy force and compelled to submit to the victor's sway.

Index

Cambridge Texts in the History of Political Thought

Titles published in the series thus far

Conciliarism and Papalism (edited by J. H. Burns and Thomas M. Izbicki)
  o 521 47674 7 paperback
Constant *Political Writings* (edited by Biancamaria Fontana)
  o 521 31632 4 paperback
Dante *Monarchy* (edited by Prue Shaw)
  o 521 56781 5 paperback
Diderot *Political Writings* (edited by John Hope Mason and Robert Wokler)
  o 521 36911 8 paperback
The Dutch Revolt (edited by Martin van Gelderen)
  o 521 39809 6 paperback
Early Greek Political Thought from Homer to the Sophists (edited by Michael Gagarin and Paul Woodruff)
  o 521 43768 7 paperback
The Early Political Writings of the German Romantics (edited by Frederick C. Beiser)
  o 521 44951 0 paperback
The English Levellers (edited by Andrew Sharp)
  o 521 62511 4 paperback
Erasmus *The Education of a Christian Prince* (edited by Lisa Jardine)
  o 521 58811 1 paperback
Fenelon *Telemachus* (edited by Patrick Riley)
  o 521 45662 2 paperback
Ferguson *An Essay on the History of Civil Society* (edited by Fania Oz-Salzberger)
  o 521 44736 4 paperback
Filmer *Patriarcha and Other Writings* (edited by Johann P. Sommerville)
  o 521 39903 3 paperback
Fletcher *Political Works* (edited by John Robertson)
  o 521 43994 9 paperback
Sir John Fortescue *On the Laws and Governance of England* (edited by Shelley Lockwood)
  o 521 58996 7 paperback
Fourier *The Theory of the Four Movements* (edited by Gareth Stedman Jones and Ian Patterson)
  o 521 35693 8 paperback
Gramsci *Pre-Prison Writings* (edited by Richard Bellamy)
  o 521 42307 4 paperback
Guicciardini *Dialogue on the Government of Florence* (edited by Alison Brown)
  o 521 45623 1 paperback
Harrington *The Commonwealth of Oceana* and *A System of Politics* (edited by J. G. A. Pocock)
  o 521 42329 5 paperback
Hegel *Elements of the Philosophy of Right* (edited by Allen W. Wood and H. B. Nisbet)
  o 521 34888 9 paperback
Hegel *Political Writings* (edited by Laurence Dickey and H. B. Nisbet)
  o 521 45979 3 paperback

Marx *Later Political Writings* (edited by Terrell Carver)
0 521 36739 5 paperback
James Mill *Political Writings* (edited by Terence Ball)
0 521 38748 5 paperback
J. S. Mill *On Liberty, with The Subjection of Women* and *Chapters on Socialism*
(edited by Stefan Collini)
0 521 37917 2 paperback
Milton *Political Writings* (edited by Martin Dzelzainis)
0 521 34866 8 paperback
Montesquieu *The Spirit of the Laws* (edited by Anne M. Cohler, Basia Carolyn
Miller and Harold Samuel Stone)
0 521 36974 6 paperback
More *Utopia* (edited by George M. Logan and Robert M. Adams)
0 521 40318 9 paperback
Morris *News from Nowhere* (edited by Krishan Kumar)
0 521 42233 7 paperback
Nicholas of Cusa *The Catholic Concordance* (edited by Paul E. Sigmund)
0 521 56773 4 paperback
Nietzsche *On the Genealogy of Morality* (edited by Keith Ansell-Pearson)
0 521 40610 2 paperback
Paine *Political Writings* (edited by Bruce Kuklick)
0 521 66799 2 paperback
Plato *The Republic* (edited by G. R. F. Ferrari and Tom Griffith)
0 521 48443 X paperback
Plato *Statesman* (edited by Julia Annas and Robin Waterfield)
0 521 44778 X paperback
Price *Political Writings* (edited by D. O. Thomas)
0 521 40969 1 paperback
Priestley *Political Writings* (edited by Peter Miller)
0 521 42561 1 paperback
Proudhon *What is Property?* (edited by Donald R. Kelley and
Bonnie G. Smith)
0 521 40556 4 paperback
Pufendorf *On the Duty of Man and Citizen according to Natural Law*
(edited by James Tully)
0 521 35980 5 paperback
The Radical Reformation (edited by Michael G. Baylor)
0 521 37948 2 paperback
Rousseau *The Discourses and other early political writings* (edited by Victor
Gourevitch)
0 521 42445 3 paperback
Rousseau *The Social Contract and other later political writings* (edited by Victor
Gourevitch)
0 521 42446 1 paperback
Seneca *Moral and Political Essays* (edited by John Cooper and John Procope)
0 521 34818 8 paperback

Sidney *Court Maxims* (edited by Hans W. Blom, Eco Haitsma Mulier and Ronald Janse)

   0 521 46736 5 paperback

Sorel *Reflections on Violence* (edited by Jeremy Jennings)

   0 521 55910 3 paperback

Spencer *The Man versus the State* and *The Proper Sphere of Government* (edited by John Offer)

   0 521 43740 7 paperback

Stirner *The Ego and Its Own* (edited by David Leopold)

   0 521 45647 9 paperback

Thoreau *Political Writings* (edited by Nancy Rosenblum)

   0 521 47675 5 paperback

Utopias of the British Enlightenment (edited by Gregory Claeys)

   0 521 45590 1 paperback

Vitoria *Political Writings* (edited by Anthony Pagden and Jeremy Lawrance)

   0 521 36714 X paperback

Voltaire *Political Writings* (edited by David Williams)

   0 521 43727 X paperback

Weber *Political Writings* (edited by Peter Lassman and Ronald Speirs)

   0 521 39719 7 paperback

William of Ockham *A Short Discourse on Tyrannical Government* (edited by A. S. McGrade and John Kilcullen)

   0 521 35803 5 paperback

William of Ockham *A Letter to the Friars Minor and other writings* (edited by A. S. McGrade and John Kilcullen)

   0 521 35804 3 paperback

Wollstonecraft *A Vindication of the Rights of Men* and *A Vindication of the Rights of Woman* (edited by Sylvana Tomaselli)

   0 521 43633 8 paperback